THE MORGAN HORSE

Jeanne Mellin

JUSTIN MORGAN

THE
Morgan Horse

JEANNE MELLIN

WITH ILLUSTRATIONS
BY THE AUTHOR

THE STEPHEN GREENE PRESS

BRATTLEBORO, VERMONT   1961

FOR JAN,

whose sparkling zest and enthusiasm
have become so very much
a part of this book.

ACKNOWLEDGMENTS

The author is grateful to the late Mr. Frank B. Hills, the Board of The Morgan Horse Club, Inc., for permission to use material from *The American Morgan Horse Register,* Mr. Seth P. Holcombe and Mr. Otho Eusey, publisher of *The Morgan Horse Magazine.* For invaluable help and encouragement thanks go, too, to: Mr. and Mrs. Gordon Voorhis, Mr. and Mrs. Kenneth Mellin, Donald J. Balch of the University of Vermont, and Messrs. Rod Leavitt, Ralph C. Lasbury Jr and Fred Herrick. For services beyond the call of duty in locating facts or illustrations the author is grateful to: Mrs. King Buckley of the Keeneland Association of Lexington, Kentucky; Miss Romana Javitz and Miss Louise Leak of the New York Public Library; Dr. Richard G. Wood, Director of the Vermont Historical Society; Mr. James J. Heslin, Director of the New-York Historical Society; Mr. A. K. Baragwanath of the Museum of the City of New York; Mr. R. L. Kolvoord of the Old Settler Bookshop, Walpole, New Hampshire; Dr. T. D. Seymour Bassett, Wilbur Librarian, the University of Vermont; Mr. Philip A. Pines, Curator of the Hall of Fame of the Trotter, and Professor John M. Kays of the University of Connecticut. Credit, again with thanks, for illustrations is given to: *The American Morgan Horse Register*—for those used on pp. 41, 43, 49, 61, 63, 87, 119, 124, 125, 128, lower 211 and 216; *The Morgan Horse Magazine*—pp. 85, 141, 157, 161, 174, 175, 196-197 (with the exceptions of Flyhawk, Windcrest Donfield and Sealect of Windcrest) and 226; the Vermont Historical Society—pp. 21, 31, 39, 70, 72, 129 and 185; the Harry T. Peters Collection of the Museum of the City of New York—pp. 52, 56 and 126; Professor Balch—pp. 208, 214, 215, 221 and 223; Mr. Voorhis—pp. 136, 145, 153, 182 and 220; Mr. Kolvoord—pp. x and 195; Mr. and Mrs. Wm. W. Barton—p. 142; Mrs. Antoinette Kelley—p. 151; Mr. and Mrs. Walter Kane—p. 176; *The Western Horseman*—both on p. 178; Leo Beckley—p. 181; Mr. and Mrs. L. S. Greenwalt—upper left p. 196; Mrs. D. D. Power—upper left p. 197, lower left p. 205; Mrs. F. O. Davis—p. 198; Mr. and Mrs. Wallace Orcutt Jr—p. 199; Mrs. Maverette Herrick—p. 201; Professor Kays—p. 222; *Eastern States Cooperator*—p. 224. Photographs and illustrations not otherwise credited are from the author's collection.

Contents

Introduction

THERE IS probably nothing more exasperating to lovers of the Morgan horse than to draw a complete blank from a listener when they mention the Morgan breed. The overwhelming ignorance and the many misconceptions concerning the Morgan are not only discouraging, they are a downright injustice to this first American breed of horse.

Anyone who knows even the minimum about horses and their respective breeds can tell you triumphantly the difference between an Arabian and, say, a Shetland pony; but mention a Morgan and your hearer is licked. Why? Certainly the Morgans have been around long enough to make themselves known. Certainly the old-timers knew all about them and praised them in their day. Why, then, the ignorance about Morgans today?

Maybe it could be blamed on the changing world, the passing of the horse 'n buggy into history. Maybe there haven't been enough Morgans in the public eye to put them on the map. But I am inclined to think that the questions so often asked about Morgans, and the erroneous statements made regarding them, come from pure lack of publicity—lack of promotion. Only a few breeders and enthusiasts have spread the word, although some horse shows have created an interest in them. Yet for anyone wishing to learn a little more about this great breed of American horse can (if no Morgan enthusiast is available from whom to get the facts) find only a minimum of widely dispersed information in a few isolated volumes.

And these casually mention the Morgan along with about every other breed going.

The only two books that are even remotely available and which have been written entirely about the Morgan are D. C. Linsley's *Morgan Horses* published in 1857, and Volume I of *The American Morgan Horse Register* published in 1894. For those who desire more detailed history of the breed and its uses today there is nothing in book form. Search as you will, fragments are all you will find. Linsley's book is rare (and expensive—if you are lucky enough to get hold of a copy) and, although its information is vital, it is limited: much took place and is taking place since it was written. The need for an up-to-date book on the Morgan horse has been long overdue. Perhaps this offering will help in some small way to fill in the gaps and enlighten both the young enthusiast as well as the serious student of the breed.

Since I am trying to give an over-all picture of the Morgan—as he was in his heyday, through his period of adjustment after the turn of the century, down to the present—there will undoubtedly be those who will take issue with some of my opinions and conclusions. To them I shall say that in every instance of possible controversy I have discussed the situation with a great number of breeders, trainers and horsemen interested in Morgans, and have let the opinions of the majority prevail.

The facts pertaining to the history of the Morgan are as correct as the limited sources of reference can make them. In places where authorities disagreed on certain facts, such as the actual birth date of Justin Morgan, I have given as far as possible either both opinions or the one which seemed most logical.

There will also be found instances where some repetition is noted. This was done for greater clarification and in some cases for stronger emphasis on a particular point. First mention of the great early Morgans is signaled by a typographic difference from the rest of the text; this device is used to differentiate Morgans from famed horses of other breeds in a number of instances, but this procedure is not followed, logically enough, in later chapters where only Morgans are under consideration.

As for illustrations, wherever possible I have included old engravings or prints for their historical value—although except for a certain ring of authenticity I feel that in many a case the artists sorely shortchanged the horse in their tortured representation of equine anatomy.

The temptation to include photographs of all up-and-coming Morgans as well as the established greats has been automatically controlled by simple lack of space. Therefore pictures of only the latter are used: the selection at this writing has a dual advantage of presenting individuals who are documented as having made their mark and who, in the case of sires, have contributed so much in establishing new lines.

My own drawings have been included for two reasons. In the case of the portrait of Justin Morgan himself I felt that it was important to present the horse pictorially according to all known descriptions available, since the early engravings have not been authenticated as having been done from life and despite their charm do not correspond to accepted data. As for the ones of Sherman, Woodbury and Bulrush, no likenesses are known to exist; these, too, have been based on painstaking study of their descriptions. And last, there are the drawings showing general and ideal aspects of the Morgan as a breed.

My aim has been to put as much information as possible about the Morgan horse under one cover and to place it in the hands of those interested in the breed. And when the day comes that I am *not* greeted with such statements as "Oh, a Morgan; isn't that some kind of work horse?" I shall feel some measure of success has been realized from my efforts.

Red Hook, New York   JEANNE MELLIN
March 1961

I

Justin Morgan

The Beginning of a Breed

NO ONE will ever know what thoughts passed through the mind of a frail singing master, Justin Morgan, as he trudged the long, lonely miles back to Randolph, Vermont, in that late summer of 1795. The big three-year-old gelding which he led and the diminutive two-year-old bay stud colt which frisked along behind undoubtedly seemed scarcely worth this trip from Randolph to West Springfield, Massachusetts. A debt owed Morgan had been paid, not in money which he so badly needed, but in these two horses instead. Surely he was far from cheery as he journeyd homeward.

The few references to this trip and the reason for it are possibly a part of the many legends which sprang up around the undersized colt which, by himself, founded the first American breed of horse—the Morgan. No accurate records have ever been found to substantiate absolutely the date of birth or the exact ancestry of the bright-eyed, high-headed colt that Justin Morgan brought home to Vermont.

In the more than 150 years since the little bay stallion toiled the fields and roads of Vermont, people interested in the breed have tried without success to trace the background of this amazing horse. They have tried to tag him Thoroughbred, Arabian, Dutch, even French (Canadian); but despite all research and endless heated arguments, no positive record has ever been found which can conclusively prove his lineage. In breeding terms he was a sport, or mutant, different from his parent stock and a type unto himself. No other

1

stallion in history has stamped his own superlative characteristics and type on his descendants so thoroughly, and he holds the exclusive distinction of having a whole new breed named in his honor. An honor he fully deserves.

It is most generally felt, and the breed *Register* goes along with this supposition, that FIGURE, as Justin Morgan called the colt which was later to bear his own name, was the son of a horse called True Briton, who was known to have traveled around under a number of assumed names, the best remembered of which was the flattering Beautiful Bay. But since the many stories and legends have made proof quite impossible, Figure's paternity will always remain a mystery.

True Briton was said to have been predominately Arabian or Thoroughbred (which in those days were similar in many respects, since the early Thoroughbred was not very far removed from the Arabian and Barb in the latter part of the eighteenth century). But, most assuredly, whatever his actual bloodlines he was a fine horse of aristocratic breeding. He was owned by Colonel James Delancey of New York. The colonel, an ardent horseman and a rather adventurous soul, took great pride in his fine stallion and availed himself of every opportunity to parade him before admiring eyes wherever they showed a spark of interest. In those early days when Americans sought good horseflesh in the same manner as we look over a showroom of shiny new automobiles, a horse of True Briton's caliber hardly went unnoticed. Delancey, unquestionably a Tory because of his decidedly Tory sympathies, naturally had many enemies among his neighbors in New York City. On several occasions his men raided local farms, running off the livestock and engaging in other mischief. This sort of behavior didn't set too well with the local inhabitants, and in retaliation a Continental soldier, finding an opportune moment, relieved the colonel of his pride and joy and skedaddled into Connecticut with True Briton. You can just bet that a horse thief's fate was probably considered much too easy and humane for this fellow; but neither he nor the horse was retrieved, so the colonel was cheated out of a fine spectacle of retribution, much to his enemies' glee.

An unknown artist's conception of Justin Morgan as it appeared in Linsley.

From here it is difficult to follow the adventures of the horse True Briton, for his name was changed on several occasions (for obvious reasons!) and he was traveled about the countryside acquiring different aliases in just about every hamlet. Traveller was one—and quite appropriate under the circumstances—and Hero was another; finally he was given the elegant name of Beautiful Bay. He was sold on one occasion to Joseph Ward of East Hartford, Connecticut, for $300, a sizable sum in those lean years, and finally fell into the hands of one Sealy Norton, also of East Hartford. It was the imaginative Mr. Norton who pinned the name Beautiful Bay on the horse and proudly stood him at stud at the stable of a John Morgan in West Springfield, Massachusetts, a mere hoot-and-a-holler from Hartford. Apparently this John Morgan was the cousin of Justin Morgan who had been late of West Springfield and had retired to Vermont in

1788. When Justin returned to West Springfield to collect on a debt owed to him by John, the latter, it seems, unloaded the gelding and the bay colt on his country cousin and, undoubtedly in the manner of most horse traders, assured Justin that they would certainly double in value with "a bit of good feed and a year's growth." We wonder whether Justin was convinced of this as he trod homeward, or whether he felt that he had been duped—and by a blood relation, too!

Another theory advanced by many researchers concerning the ancestry of the colt Justin reluctantly led home, was that he was a Dutch horse and, using the vernacular of the day, of "the best blood." Justin Morgan was alleged to have always referred to the colt, which he always called Figure, as being a Dutch horse, although the only thing to substantiate this idea is the fact that there was a Dutch stallion standing in Springfield in 1792. It was quite possible that Figure's dam was brought to the court of this horse, whose name was Young Bulrock, and who was large and a bright bay in color. Most of the so-called Dutch horses were described as being of light draft type with short legs and heavy bodies, and having thick manes and tails and quite a bit of hair about the fetlocks. (Does this sound like the description of an Arabian horse? Well, the Dutch horses were said to be largely of grade Arabian stock! One wonders what the other half was!)

Now, the date of Figure's birth—which everyone argues about but no one can prove—at first glance would seemingly determine his breeding. If, as some would have us believe, he was by True Briton (or, if you will, Beautiful Bay), it is quite likely that he was foaled in 1789, because that worthy animal was known to have been standing at stud for the seasons of 1788-89. On the other hand, if he was indeed by Young Bulrock, the Dutch horse, his foaling date would more than likely be about 1793. This date seems to tie in better if we are to believe that Justin Morgan made his historic trip to Springfield in 1795, when the colt was supposedly two years old.

About his dam everyone seems to agree—to which we say "Amen." She was described as a "native of the Connecticut Valley," which, if you are a student of geography, you know takes in quite a hunk of territory; but which we assume in this case means in and around Hartford, Springfield and vicinity. She was called the "Wildair mare," and was supposedly of the same blood as True Briton—Arabian or Barb. Her sire, called Diamond, definitely had an "imported from England" background. We raise an eyebrow at his description, however, as it doesn't put one in mind of either Thoroughbred or Arabian breeding. He was of middle size—which isn't much help, since we're not certain what was then considered large and small—and heavy-bodied, with a thick, bushy mane and tail. He was called a smooth traveler (this might tally with Arabian blood), a trait which he is said to have bestowed upon his daughter, the Wildair mare, Figure's dam. She was a light bay in color and of medium size, having long hair on her legs and fetlocks and a bushy mane and tail like her father's. She was undoubtedly a good-looking mare and a good mover from all indications.

Yet despite all this conjecture about Figure's parents, his lineage actually matters very little now. For he was an outstanding horse himself and the beginning of a distinctive new breed. He was Adam to the Morgan breed, and no one can deny that those who came after him were far more important than those who came before.

HIS APPEARANCE

Figure's arrival in the little settlement of Randolph, Vermont, was presumably taken quite lightly at first. Indeed, one needs little imagination to conjure up the reactions of the townsfolk when Justin arrived home with his unexpected horse companions. A mere pony in size, his bay colt was just a mite too small for the work expected of a horse in that rugged countryside—or so quoth the local experts. "The gelding might be good for something," they allowed, "but that little runt ain't worth a hill o' beans. Sure as sap flows in the spring, skiddin' logs ain't for ponies." And Justin Morgan's new colt fell neatly into the pony category. So you see Figure scarcely took Randolph by storm. But it wouldn't be long before he put the big horses to shame all around the town, in a variety of ways, too.

The most accurate description of Figure made him about 14 hands high and weighing about 950 pounds. He was a rich, dark bay, with

Dyberry Billy shows how Justin's stamp endures.

the customary black legs, mane and tail. There wasn't a white hair on him, and his mane and tail were coarse and heavy with no tendency to curl (this last could be an Arabian characteristic). His head was good but, contrary to some notions, it was not extremely small. However it was lean, bony and very clean-cut. His profile was straight, with a broad forehead, and his ears were very small and fine and set wide apart. His best feature was his very dark and prominent eyes. The expression in them was spirited but pleasant, and no white showed around the edge of the lids.

In conformation Figure was as distinctive as a race horse is from a Percheron, yet he resembled neither. His body was rather long, due to the extreme depth of shoulders and the powerfully muscled and long quarters. He was close-ribbed; his back was short from wither to loin, and his barrel was very round and deep with no tendency to lightness in the flanks. His chest was wide and deep, projecting a good deal in front. The crest of his neck was high-arched and deeply muscled, an outstanding characteristic which has been a true Morgan feature through the years. The symmetry that this cresty neck, deep, well-rounded body and high-carried head gives the Morgan, is an appearance that is identifiable as Morgan in any group of horses.

Figure's legs were short and close-joined, with flat bone that was completely free from coarseness, although his fetlocks were a bit hairy. At all seasons of the year, however, his coat was soft and glossy, without the exceeding heaviness often seen on horses where the climate is cold at some season.

The remarkable point to remember as you read the description of Figure is that it tallies so closely with many modern Morgans today except for the matter of size—which even in his sons was varied. It is remarkable, considering that the average Morgan nowadays carries only about 10 percent of Figure's blood, that the stamp of his fabulous progenitor is present still, and is as recognizable as it was in the earliest days of the breed.

HIS PROWESS

From the very moment that he was fitted into a work harness, Figure's life was one work-a-day task after another. And work in that time and place was from dawn till dusk. Even so, Figure's day's work didn't always end when the sun had slipped down behind the Green Mountains.

By the time he was about four years old Figure really knew what the pinch of a collar and the tug of trace chains meant. For Justin, always in dire straits moneywise, leased him out to a local farmer named Robert Evans for $15 a year, a sum for which the little horse was put to work clearing a hillside woodlot. And the hillside woodlots in Vermont are rock gardens in the most literal sense of the word: they are so steep and rough that it almost seems that the unrelenting soil is staging a bitter tug of war with the men who come to till it. Into the woods, then, went Figure with a farmer at the lines who, I'm sure, was very dubious about the ability of his "team"—the team being Figure alone. But imagine his astonishment when he discovered that his pint-sized companion was a veritable dynamo of energy and strength!

No secret is ever a secret very long in a small village, and it was

only a matter of the time it takes to fill a skidway that Figure's prowess in the woodlot made a topic of conversation around the general store of an evening. "He's right handy—might just amount to somethin' after all." It wasn't long at all before it was common knowledge that Morgan's horse, Figure, made up in ability and spirit for what he lacked in size.

One story that sprang from who knows where, but one which an actual eyewitness, Nathan Nye, claims is true, every bit of it, was the account of a test of strength among the village horses. It concerns an occasion when a particularly large pine log was defying all comers to pull it from its resting place near the sawmill in Randolph. All the local horses had found it just too heavy for their liking, and failed at all attempts to skid the log even one foot. Finally, down the street at dusk came Evans with the little bay stallion. He was just returning from a full day's labor on his piece of property over the ridge;

but when he heard that there was a little logging still left undone in the village, he chirruped to Figure and strode down to see what was what. His confidence in the horse knew no bounds, so, sizing up the situation, he challenged the whole company gathered to see the sport, betting a gallon of spirits (in this case rum) that Figure could draw the log onto the way in three pulls. Now, Vermonters are always game for a little harmless diversion. Laughing and scoffing, they accepted the challenge. "Not even the Runt can budge that piece of timber," they said, for even though Figure was known by all as a resolute puller, this was asking just too much of the little fellow. Good-naturedly they heckled Evans as he fastened the tug chains to the log. But now Evans, a bit miffed at their jokes at his expense, stated that he was ashamed to hitch his horse to such a small log, and if three stout men would sit astride it, he would forfeit the rum if Figure didn't draw it at least ten rods. Agreeable to anything at this point, three of the brawniest men present clambered onto the log while Nathan Nye held the lantern in the gathering darkness. Warning the men to look out for their legs, Evans snapped up the lines and roared to Figure, "Git up!" The stallion instantly bent his mighty neck, straining into the collar. The laughing crowd grew silent as the swelling, powerful muscles flexed and rippled under the satin coat. With a mighty lunge, Figure, all his weight leaning into the harness, started the log. A cheer arose as, drawing it and the men, he didn't stop until he had gone halfway the distance to the sawmill. In the next pull he landed the load at the spot agreed upon.

Morgan's horse Figure had many an admirer after that night. Having worked hard in the fields and woods all day, he had outdrawn all the horses in the village that same evening!

But not only at pulling did Figure excel. Evans knew a good thing when he had it, and he had it in the bay stallion. He would ride the stallion into the village in the evenings with the work of the day behind him, looking for some form of relaxation. It might have been relaxation for him, but it certainly wasn't for the little horse. There was always some challenge floating around unanswered, or some record to beat. It mattered little whether the proposal was for a race at the trot or the gallop, or even at the walk: he would always accept on Figure's behalf. And he won with regularity. Up and down the countryside the horse gained fame. "Morgan's horse," people said, "can toil all day and win races at dusk!"

D. C. Linsley in his *Morgan Horses,* published in 1857, gives a stirring description of Figure (called by his later and well-known name throughout the book), and the type of races he won. Because the facts are interesting and the book is rare, a portion of the text is quoted here:

"He [Figure, or Justin Morgan] was a fleet runner at short distances. Running horses short distances for small stakes was very common in Vermont fifty years ago. Eighty rods was very generally the length of the course, which usually commenced at a tavern or grocery and extended the distance agreed upon, up or down the public road. In these races the horses were started from a 'scratch,' that is, a mark was drawn across the road in the dirt, and the horses, ranged in a row upon it, went off at 'the drop of a hat' or some other signal. It will be observed that the form of Justin Morgan was not such as in our days is thought best calculated to give the greatest speed for a short distance. Those who believe in long-legged racers will think his legs, body and stride were too short, and to them it may perhaps seem surprising that he should be successful, as he invariably was, in such contests. But we think his great muscular development and nervous energy, combined with his small size, gave him a decided advantage in the first start over taller and heavier horses; just as any ordinary horse can distance the finest locomotive in a ten rod race. At all events, the history of racing in this country and in England, proves conclusively that small horses may have great speed. In such a race a horse of great spirit and nervous energy derives a decided advantage from these qualities, especially after being a little accustomed to such struggles. When brought up to the line, his [Justin Morgan's or Figure's] eyes flash and his ears quiver with intense excitement, he grinds the bit with his teeth, his hind legs are drawn under him, every muscle of his frame trembles and swells almost to bursting and at the given signal he goes off like the spring of a steel trap. His unvarying success in these short races may perhaps be partly accounted for in this way, though he was undoubtedly possessed of more than ordinary speed, and was a sharp runner."

So far afield did Figure's fame spread that on at least one occasion two Thoroughbreds were imported to race against him. In Brookfield, Vermont, so the records show, on June 26, 1796, Figure accepted the challenge from a horse called Sweepstakes, brought to the small Vermont town all the way from Long Island. Also, another horse, a gray mare called Silvertail from St. Lawrence County, New York, was to try her luck against his.

Everyone gathered at the little country track feared that this time Morgan's horse had met his match. Nevertheless the cheers were with him, even if the money might have rested elsewhere. The distance of the race, or, as it turned out races, was eighty rods; not a long race but probably all the primitive little track would allow. The most interesting thing was, however, that Figure was to take on each of his challengers separately! Now, both challengers were used and trained solely for racing, having no other use in life; yet here was the small Vermont logging horse going to take them both on—one at a time.

Imagine the great surprise and chagrin of the racing men when the diminutive work horse from the back country of Vermont soundly beat both their champions handily! Morgan is said even to have given the defeated parties a chance to win back some of their losses by matching their horses against Figure in a walking race and/ or a trotting race if they preferred, but undoubtedly they'd seen about enough of Figure's heels and declined any further sport. Without a doubt there was much celebrating by the Vermonters that evening.

When Robert Evans's lease on Figure was up, the stallion was returned reluctantly to the stable of the singing master, Justin Morgan. It was on the back of this dashing young horse that the sickly Morgan, racked with consumption, made his rounds to teach music and singing in the little villages around Randolph. In those days people considered it of prime importance that their chidren learn singing as well as the 3 R's, and they allotted funds to pay the singing master to come to their community. Thus on many a blustery day Justin Morgan, old in health if not in years, rode out into the countryside, earning his small, much-needed fees. The sprightly Figure carried him easily over the miles, and many travelers on the road could recall seeing the wasted man and his robust little stallion moving away down the empty roads as he went about his lonely rounds during the winters of 1796, '97 and '98.

But Justin's health had been growing steadily worse, and on March 22, 1798, he fought back no longer. Since his wife had died and his family had been split up into foster homes, Morgan, during his last illness before his death, lived with Sheriff Rice, a friend in Woodstock. It was to this man that he gave his well-loved young stallion as payment for expenses incurred while he was ill in the sheriff's house.

The town records of Randolph show that Justin Morgan left no valuable papers or documents to reveal answers to the tantalizing questions about the original Morgan horse. Indeed, all his worldly goods at the time of his death amounted to the pitiful sum of $160.13. Thus passed the simple Vermonter who will be remembered not for great deeds, but because he once owned a little bay stallion he called Figure. He had written many hymns, some of which were published and can be found in old collections of sacred music, but these have long since passed out of use. Yet the breed of horse established under his name yearly increases in numbers and popularity.

HIS FAME AS JUSTIN MORGAN

It was after the death of the singing master that Figure became known as "the Justin Morgan horse" and, finally, as simply JUSTIN MORGAN. His days were to be filled with endless hard work and a succession of owners both good and bad.

Sheriff Rice of Woodstock found a number of chores for the Morgan horse to do when he owned him, and the young stallion found no slackening of pace with his change of ownership. The sheriff, however, gave him good care during the years that he was in his barn. But old Bob Evans had his eye on the horse, biding his time until the stallion might come up for sale. He'd never had another horse like him before—or since!—and needless to say he was itching to get his hands on the Morgan again if the opportunity ever presented itself. His chance came sooner than he thought: the sheriff decided to sell, and back to the Randolph woods went the bay stallion, to labor from dawn to dusk without respite.

Not only were his hours in harness as long and tiring as they had been before, but the old racing and pulling bees were as frequent as ever. His reputation firmly established, he was attracting much attention now as a sire, and folks began to bring their mares to him. And what a varied lot they were! Draft mares of Canadian blood, big mares, small mares, sound mares and lame mares; mares of all colors and types were brought to the Morgan, who was expected to perform miracles. And he did not disappoint the owners of this varied group, for the foals that arrived each spring resembled their dams not at all, but their sire. The farmers and the horsemen—even the young folks who had been allowed to borrow the family mare to raise a colt from—were delighted. Regardless of the conformation of the mare they had hopefully sent to Justin Morgan, the foals always resembled their dad! They had the same round, close-coupled bodies, the same bold expression, the same sprightly gait and, best of all, the same gentle disposition.

For a number of years this situation remained unchanged, and the little stallion enjoyed the admiration and respect of the countryside.

Then everything changed. Robert Evans, not making quite as much of a success of his business as the horse was making of *his,* fell into bankruptcy, was sued for debt in 1804, and was put in the pokey. Colonel John Goss, a good man and a keen judge of horses, took the Morgan horse as security against Evans's bail; by paying the farmer's debts he became the legal owner of the stallion.

Under his new owner, Justin Morgan's horse continued his previous occupations and, although worked as long and as hard, was given good care and wasn't abused. As well as the usual farm work which was his daily lot, he was ridden and evidently driven occasionally for pleasure as well. Linsley gives a brief insight into this other facet of the Morgan's life with this description, which I think is worth quoting here:

"His proud, bold and fearless style of movement and his vigorous, untiring action, have, perhaps, never been surpassed. When a rider was on him, he was obedient to the slightest motion of the rein, would walk backward rapidly under a gentle pressure of the bit and moved side-ways almost as willingly as he moved forward; in short, was perfectly trained to all the paces and evolutions of a parade horse; and when ridden at military reviews (as was frequently the case) his bold, imposing style, and spirited, nervous action attracted universal attention and admiration. He was perfectly gentle and kind to handle and loved to be groomed and caressed, but he disliked to have children about him and had an inveterate hatred for dogs, if loose always chasing them out of sight the instant he saw them. When taken out with a halter or bridle he was in constant motion and very playful."

LAST YEARS

In 1811 little Justin Morgan's luck began running out, and he came onto the proverbial hard times. How often we wonder how a horse of his obvious greatness could have been so unappreciated as to have been served as he was! It has always seemed cruel and heartless that he was made constantly to suffer in the closing years of his life, with no compassionate person to rescue him from the rigors and hardships of the life he was forced to lead. There was Jacob Sanderson, who bought him in 1811 and then sold him. There was William Langmaid, a cruel taskmaster who used the aging little stallion in a six-horse hitch hauling freight between Windsor and Chelsea. How unfeeling and dull these men must have been to subject not only a well-known horse but an old one as well, to the afflictions of the road! Treated roughly, with no regard for past performances or fame, the Morgan horse became poor and worn; when he could be of no further use he was again sold down the road, this time for a pitifully small sum, to a man in Chelsea. A succession of owners followed, each seemingly anxious to pass him along for fear he would die on their hands. He returned to Randolph around 1816 under the ownership of a Samuel Stone, but after two or three years he left his old home for good and was kept at the farm of Clifford Bean, about three miles south of the village of Chelsea. It was here that he was to end his days.

Turned out in a small pasture with other horses to shift for himself without benefit of shelter or care, he was kicked in the flank by one of his companions. Since no one apparently saw or cared what happened to him, his injury was left unattended and inflammation set in. Alone and completely unmourned, in 1821 old Justin Morgan breathed his last. He was about thirty years old when death ended his suffering.

It is a sad note indeed that the sole founder of America's first great breed of horse should come to his end in this manner, but the legacy he left behind him in the many sons and daughters cast in his image has spread his fame from ocean to ocean and to other lands.

"Before receiving the injury which caused his death," Linsley says, "the Morgan horse was completely sound and free from any description of blemish despite his amazingly arduous life. His limbs were perfectly smooth and free from any swelling and very limber and supple.

"Those who saw him in 1819 and 1820, describe his appearance as remarkably fresh and youthful. Age had not quenched his spirit, nor dampened the ardor of his temper; years of severest labor had not sapped his vigor, nor broken his constitution; his eye was still bright and his step firm and elastic."

II

Sons of Justin Morgan

ALTHOUGH there were undoubtedly many direct sons of old Justin Morgan (as we shall refer to the stallion henceforth), no authentic account of more than six which were *kept at stud* in New England has ever been found, despite endless research into the subject undertaken by students of the breed.

D. C. Linsley was the most noted authority on the subject of the origins of the Morgans, and the facts he unearthed during his lifetime have been invaluable to anyone and everyone interested in the breed. He states, concerning the sons of Justin Morgan:

"Between all the stallions left by him there was a very close and striking resemblance, in size, form, and general character, and they also bore equal resemblance to their sire; indeed, the power of transmitting to his progeny his own form, constitution and temperament, was a very distinguishing trait of Justin Morgan, and we believe no horse ever lived that possessed in a higher degree the power of stamping upon his offspring his own great leading characteristics."

Justin Morgan's important characteristics, which he passed on to his sons were: his compactness of form; his high and generous spirit, combined with the most perfect gentleness and tractability, and his sinewy limbs, his lofty style and his easy but vigorous action.

The fact that not only did his valuable qualities descend unimpaired to the next generation, but apparently with little diminution to the second and third, thus establishing a new breed of horse, makes Justin Morgan undeniably just about the most important

16

horse ever foaled in America. His legacy was the fine and enduring breed which helped to develop New England, and subsequently all America.

Although many other stallions sired by Justin were kept for breeding, the four which became most celebrated were SHERMAN, WOODBURY, BULRUSH and REVENGE. These four, with the HAWKINS HORSE and the FENTON HORSE, were the sons of old Justin whom Linsley was able to trace with accuracy. Possibly other sons of Justin were just as valuable or well known in their own time and place, but often fate deals with a horse unfavorably, so that he is lost in obscurity though he may possess all the qualities for fame. Such seems to have been the fate of the unknown sons of old Justin, and they have remained anonymous through the years.

Without any doubt the three most important sons of Justin Morgan were Sherman, Woodbury and Bulrush, and since each was responsible for a family in his own right much more detail is known about the lives of these three. Each became the progenitor of an immediate family, with his descendants being bred back to produce *third and fourth generation* horses more like the original Justin Morgan than any of his sons. Perhaps because the mares which produced them were so dissimilar, each of the three was known for his distinction from the others.

That the important features that characterize Justin Morgan were strongly and strikingly impressed upon his offspring, can be seen in the following descriptions of his known sons. Yet not only did his unique qualities go almost full strength to the next generation, but apparently they did so practically undiluted to the second and third. Where pains were taken to select both sires and dams possessing most of his blood and characteristics, the resulting foals closely resembled Justin in all important respects—except, perhaps, in size, in which there was a decided increase.

SHERMAN

The first of the three most outstanding sons of Justin Morgan was Sherman. It was felt by many that Sherman was the greatest of them all, for he sired a prominent line down through BLACK HAWK 20 and his son ETHAN ALLEN 50. His daughters, when bred to his half-brothers Bulrush and Woodbury, contributed greatly to the success of the Morgan breed.

Because he was a highly esteemed horse in his own day, it is a matter of some interest that the actual birth date of Sherman is not known. Consensus seems to put it either 1808 or 1809.

Appearance and Early Years

By way of description, Sherman was a bright red chestnut, standing slightly under 14 hands and weighing about 925 pounds. His off hind leg was white from the foot halfway to the hock, and he had a small white stripe in his face. His head was lean and well shaped, with small, fine ears; and his eyes, although inclined to be small, were prominent and lively. He had the legs of his sire, including the same long hair at the fetlocks and the back of his cannons. He had an excellent deep chest with the prominent breastbone similar to his sire's, while his shoulders were large and well laid back into good withers. His neck was well crested and embellished with a full mane, but one not so heavy as Justin's. He had quarters which were long and deep, with broad and muscular loins. He was, however, a bit hollow-backed, a trait which occasionally he passed on to his get. But this tendency never seemed to indicate a weak back, for the horse worked hard all his life and never suffered from any weakness or breaking down.

Sherman's dam was a mare of high quality, some records stating that she was a full-blooded Spanish Barb. She was a light chestnut with a star, strip and snip, and three white legs. She stood over 15 hands. Her head was good; ears small, neck rather thin and long. She always carried her head high, exhibiting a marked degree of high-spiritedness, although her nature seemed pleasant enough. She was a good mare in harness, but seemingly at her best under saddle, and was used at the latter by most of her owners.

When brought from Rhode Island to Vermont by John Sherman, the mare unfortunately slipped her hip and was never quite sound again. She was subsequently given to his brother James of Lyndon, Vermont. James's son, George Sherman, was given the colt resulting

from the crossing of this mare with Justin Morgan. This was in 1811, when the colt was three years old.

George Sherman was a hard-working man, and the horses in his keeping were compelled to keep their noses to the proverbial grindstone as he did. Like his sire, Sherman, only a pony in size, was required to labor long and hard at work meant for horses twice his size. Beginning at the age of four he was worked singly, and occasionally in a team with a large brown draft mare, on the stoneboat and at pulling stumps. But also like his sire, he never shirked any work asked of him, and was always willing and agreeable.

In the winter Sherman usually ran a team steadily between Lyndon and Portland, Maine. For several years this team consisted of Sherman and a half-brother by Justin Morgan who was a year older and a bit larger. This horse never gained the fame of his brother, never being named and probably never used at stud. Little is known of him except that he was a son of old Justin and was a heavier and slightly coarser horse than Sherman. Along the route between Lyndon and Portland, George Sherman was known as a man who would never be outdone in any kind of sport or wager, especially anything involving horses. He was always ready to match his team against any he met, either to draw or run, for a small wager. And his little team soon became famous at every inn on the route.

The races were always at catch weights, and usually for the distance of about eighty rods or about a quarter of a mile. As in Justin's time, the starting line was a scratch drawn across the road, and at the given signal the horses were off. Sherman soon became as adept at this sport as his sire had been, being alert and eager and able to reach his full stride in a matter of a few feet. It wasn't very long before other teamsters became reluctant to match their horses against the Morgans, and only strangers who hadn't heard of George Sherman and his team offered any competition.

Record at Stud

Such was the life of Sherman Morgan from his fourth year until he was about ten. At this time he was sold to Stephen C. Gibbs of Littleton, New Hampshire, to be used at the stud. He remained

A stud poster extols the virtues of Sherman's line.

there for three seasons; afterwards he was traveled extensively by various owners around the Granite State, and many a stud poster tacked on a livery stable wall advertised the qualifications of Sherman Morgan. After several prolific seasons in New Hampshire, Sherman was returned to Vermont in the ownership of John Buckminster of Danville, who also stood the horse at stud in St. Johnsbury and Danville in 1828.

In 1829 he returned to Littleton with John Bellows as his owner and Gibbs providing the stable and care. He became a well-liked and highly regarded stallion—never unappreciated, as Justin had been during his lifetime.

For five more years under the ownership of Bellows, Sherman Morgan sired fine foundation stock of the breed that was to sweep New England and the growing America. Bellows stood the horse each season in a different location and was known to have leased Sherman every season to a qualified person who could handle the stud and take the responsibility of him. In 1830 he stood in Dover, New Hampshire, and vicinity; in 1831 he was at Colonel Jacques's Ten Hills Farm in Charlestown, Massachusetts. The colonel, liking the horse and the colts sired by him very much, tried to persuade Bellows to let him keep the stallion another season. However he failed to do so, and this fact and Sherman's making the season of 1832 in Dover, Durham and South Berwick, New Hampshire, instead, resulted in the stud's being bred to the mare that produced his best son, Black Hawk 20.

In 1833 and 1834 he remained in the vicinity of Dover. Records state that he sired twenty-seven foals in 1833. In 1834, his last year, he was bred to fifty-seven mares, but no record can be found of the number of live foals resulting.

Sherman Morgan was probably the most popular of old Justin's sons, and the family he founded was very much like the old horse himself. His offspring were very tractable and easily broken to any use. They had their sire's short, nervous step and were also tough and courageous. That some of them also inherited their sire's hollow back could never be considered too much of a fault, as no weakness was ever apparent from this cause. Of his twenty sons left stallions, most were chestnut, although there were several grays, bays and blacks, and one brown. His other offspring were generally chestnut, with white markings on face and legs quite common. They ranged in height from 13.2-15.2, the average being 14.3.

Sherman Morgan died January 9, 1835, in the stable of John Bellows in Lancaster, New Hampshire. The actual cause of his death is unknown, although a heart attack was suspected. After appearing as usual in the morning, he was found dead in his stall shortly after one o'clock in the afternoon. With the exception of some slight indications of age, he was apparently as free from every species of blemish or infirmity on the morning of his death as on the day when he was foaled.

In stature Sherman was small, but like his sire he had a heart as big as the Green Mountain country in which he was foaled.

WOODBURY

If little Sherman Morgan was the hard-working, even-tempered individual of the known sons of Justin, then Woodbury could be called the show horse of the group, for he really enjoyed an opportunity to strut his stuff. He especially relished the noise and confusion attendant to the old Vermont muster days. The martial music and the flag-waving were meant for him, one would think, to see the horse on one of these occasions. He had absolutely no fear of the flashing uniforms or the pounding drums, but would prance and parade to the delight of all, and never was there a muster or a ceremony which he attended where he would go unnoticed.

Woodbury, at 14.3, was the largest of the three, and with his bold, fearless and showy ways seemed more like his sire than any of the others.

Qualities and Background
In color he was a rich, dark chestnut, with a white stocking on his off hind leg and an oddly shaped blaze on his face which ran from his upper lip to a little more than halfway to his eyes with no white between his eyes at all. He was a very compact horse with a broad chest, deep quarters and an excellent back and loin. His croup was

nearly level with a high-set tail, which, after the fashion of the day, had been docked and was only ten inches long. His head was small and lean, bespeaking quality, and his large dark hazel eyes were set far apart and were very prominent and bright. His face was straight, his nostrils were very large and full, and he had the tiny ears that were to become such a positive characteristic of the Morgan breed.

In action Woodbury was very bold and fiery, with a nervous temperament that never allowed him to stand still. When led out in a bridle, he was restive and playful, tossing his head and dancing about and never seeming to be without motion. Surprisingly, he was good in harness despite his nervousness, but it was said that he always appeared at his best under saddle. Militia colonels and generals were always eager to ride him at the musters or reviews, for his showiness was also coupled with a pleasant disposition.

Woodbury was foaled the latter part of May 1816 in Tunbridge, Vermont, and was the property of Lyman Wight. He, too, had a couple of aliases, being sometimes called "the Burbank horse," and in Windsor County he was known as "the Walker horse."

Nothing has ever been learned about the blood of his dam. At the time the colt was foaled, Wight was a young man, about eighteen years old, and the mare belonged to his father, William Wight, who lent her to his son for the purpose of raising a colt. Woodbury's dam was five years old when he was foaled. She was a large mare for those days, standing over 15 hands and weighing about 1,100 pounds. In color she was a deep bay with black points, and had a small star in her forehead but no other white markings. Although not very compactly built and with a tendency to be flat-ribbed, she nevertheless had an excellent chest, fine shoulders and good quarters. Her head, which was very fine, she carried high. She was known to be "good on the road and with a turn of speed." She nevertheless had a tendency to pace as well as trot (oh, how it's frowned upon in this day and age!), but she did not seem to pass this trait on to her son, nor did Woodbury's get show any inclination to pace. It was said that she made a fine appearance when trotting and attracted much attention for her speed.

At weaning time the colt was sold by Wight to David Woodbury

of Bethel, Vermont, for the sum of $50. Woodbury kept the young stallion until he was mature and trained him for both saddle and harness before selling him to his brother John.

Reputation and Travels

John Woodbury was known as a keen judge of horses, and his new horse caused quite a stir in the community. For several seasons John kept the stallion at stud in Bethel and surrounding towns, where his get became quite favorably known.

When John Woodbury sold his horse to Ebenezer Parkhurst, the price received was high for those days. Parkhurst kept the stud until he was ten years old before selling him to Simon Smith and William Walker in March 1826. The price tag this time was $500. Shortly afterwards, Smith and Walker dissolved partnership and Walker became the sole owner of Woodbury.

Because Walker had a passion for horses and recognized the fact that Woodbury's fine qualities were inherited from his sire, Justin Morgan, he went to great pains to have the Morgan stock brought into the limelight. Unfortunately, after owning Woodbury only four years, the man's assets were too meager to make the venture pay, and he was forced to sacrifice the stallion for, in his own words, "the insignificant sum of four hundred dollars."

Woodbury's new owner was Peter Burbank, a lawyer of Newbury, Vermont. Burbank was not a breeder but was very fond of horses, and having seen Woodbury on one occasion at Keene, New Hampshire, became very taken with the horse and wished to buy him. He had a discriminating eye and knew a horse's good points. Still, he did not trust his own judgment, and consulted Jesse Johnson of Bradford, Vermont, about the advisability of buying the horse. Now, Johnson was an astute horseman with a close, critical eye that could take in at a glance all the minute defects of form that a more careless observer might fail to discover. However upon seeing Woodbury, he was quite aware of the stallion's merit, and wholeheartedly advised Burbank to purchase the horse; which he did on the 20th of May 1830.

For six years the Johnson brothers of Bradford had charge of old

Woodbury and he was kept at their stables during the winter and the latter part of the summer and autumn of each year, and, for one or two years, kept there all year round. He also stood at stud in Keene, New Hampshire, and Burlington, Vermont.

When Burbank died in September 1836, the administrators of his estate decided that the horse must be sold. It can be easily imagined that there were many regrets when the well-known and well-liked Woodbury was sold at auction in Wells River, Vermont, only to be shipped away from his native state to Gainesville, Alabama.

He was purchased by Norman Baglee of that town and sent to sea aboard a small sailing packet from Boston. The trip was very rough and exceedingly unpleasant and Woodbury fared badly, arriving in Alabama in extremely poor condition. It is related that he unloaded with much difficulty from the boat, and some accounts state that he slipped and broke a leg at the time. This has never been verified, however, and seems rather unlikely as the horse lived two years more in Alabama. But he never regained his health and one wonders if the spirit he had always possessed had departed, too. There is no evidence of his leaving any stock at all in Alabama before his death at the age of twenty-two in 1838.

BULRUSH

All three of the outstanding sons of Justin Morgan were used in about the same capacity all their lives and were similar to their sire in many ways, yet each left his own mark on the breed known as Morgan, and Bulrush was no exception.

Bulrush was foaled in 1812 and, again like the others, little is known about his dam. She was a dark bay with a heavy black mane and tail; she was built low to the ground, compact, and had heavy limbs with large joints. Her neck was rather long and, though her head was good, she did not carry it high. She was a fast trotter but inclined to be lacking in spirit. Her appearance indicated that she was of French (Canadian) blood and she was said to be probably of this breeding.

At the time Bulrush was sired, she was owned by Moses Belknap of Randolph, Vermont. Belknap was known to have obtained her from a teamster from Montpelier by the name of Boutwell, who had worked her in a six-horse hitch hauling merchandise and produce between Montpelier and Boston. Even though the mare was rugged and hardy, with great endurance, Boutwell thought her too small for his business, and he exchanged her with Belknap for a larger horse.

Late in the winter, when the mare was heavy in foal to Justin Morgan, Belknap sold her to Ziba Gifford of Tunbridge. The deal that went with her was that Gifford was to keep the foal until it was four months old, and then return it to Belknap; or, if he wished, he could keep the colt and pay $13 for it. Thirteen dollars for a Morgan foal—and by Justin, too! But evidently Gifford was short of cash, for he chose to return the colt.

Belknap kept Bulrush in Tunbridge and vicinity until 1819. At an early age the young stallion was broken to harness and saddle

and he became a popular stud in the countryside around Tunbridge, leaving many sons and daughters there. The uniformity of type and tremendous endurance of his offspring gained him much patronage.

Like Sherman, Bulrush was a small horse, standing only 14 hands and weighing about 1,000 pounds. He was a dark bay in color with a few white hairs on the forehead, but no other white at all. His black mane and tail were exceedingly heavy and coarse: he must have made quite a picture, as it was said that his mane came down nearly to his knees, while his forelock fell to the tip of his nose! His tail had been docked when he was a colt, yet the hair was bushy and full even though short in length. His legs, like Justin's, were large, powerfully muscled and had the feathering of hair at the back of the cannon. His back, while not so short as either Sherman's or Woodbury's, was broad and straight, with no inclination to be hollow as the others' were. He was very deep in the chest, with shoulders which were powerful though possibly not so well placed.

Speed and Endurance

Although Bulrush lacked Woodbury's boldness and proud manner, and the short, nervous step of his brother, he was a sharp and speedy horse in harness, and indeed a faster horse at the trot than either Sherman or Woodbury. He was said to be a bit cross at times, but in harness this tendency rarely showed itself. His most outstanding trait, however, was his remarkable endurance. In this he had no equal, and all the local folk were well aware of the fact when sending their mares to be bred to him.

Of all Justin's sons, Bulrush probably got a more uniform group of colts, for they resembled their sire in color, type and weight. They were almost all dark bay or brown without white markings, and never a chestnut or sorrel. Almost all of them, too, had the same thick, luxurious mane and tail, and were extraordinarily good-legged and hardy.

Standing in New England

In his lifetime Bulrush had many owners and traveled around his native state and neighboring New Hampshire much the same way as

BOXER!

Boxer is 5 years old the 1st of May, 1871, is of a dark Bay color, with a heavy black main and tail, stands 16 hands high and weighs 1135 lbs.

Boxer was sired by Smith Morrill, known as the "Hutchinson Horse," and he by the old original Morrill. Boxer's dam was a Morgan mare sired by the young Bulrush, and he by the old Bulrush, this giving him as much Morgan blood as any horse in the State. Boxer's sire is a great and noble horse, weighs 1300 lbs., and has trotted his full mile in 2.44, quicker time than ever was made by any horse of his weight in the State. Boxer is a favorite with all lovers of good horses for his style, build, and speed, and is pronounced the best five years old stallion that stands in Vermont; also, I stand ready to match him with any horse of his age and weight, for trotting or roading, or any other points I have mentioned about him.

Boxer will stand for the use of mares the coming season, at J. Woodward's stable, So. Royalton, Vt.,

On _____

TERMS: $10 TO WARRANT, OR $6 SINGLE LEAP.

All mares at a distance shall be well cared for, and kept in good pastures, for $1 per week, at the owner's risk.

NOTICE.

I propose to have a show of Boxer stock Sept. 23, 1871, at South Royalton, Vt., for the purpose of paying a premium to the best yearling colt, and the best sucking colt, on that day, Sept. 23. Owners of said stock shall choose three disinterested men for their judges to decide on the best colts. Premiums to be paid by the services of the Horse. The best one year old colt, $6; second best, $3. The best sucking colt, $6; second best, $3.

J. WOODWARD, Owner.

South Royalton, Vt., June 12, 1871.

Argus and Patriot Job Printing House, Montpelier, Vt.

Bulrush blood promises stamina for Boxer's get.

old Justin had; always leaving behind him the finest of stock to aid in the development of a new and growing land.

Some of his owners included the same partnership of Smith and Walker which had owned his brother Woodbury. When this partnership dissolved and Walker became the sole owner of Woodbury, Smith kept Bulrush. After a season in Maidstone, Vermont, and two years in the State of Maine, Bulrush was sold in 1833 to Jesse Johnson of Bradford, Vermont, where he was stabled with his brother Woodbury, then owned by Burbank. In 1833 Bulrush made a circuit season between Bradford and Bath, New Hampshire; 1834 found him in Keene, a hundred miles away. In 1835 he stood in Lyme, also in New Hampshire, and then back to Bradford. The next season found him far in the western part of Vermont in Burlington. Considering that there were no means of horse transportation as we know it today, and a horse went everywhere on its own power, it is an undisputed fact that little Bulrush scarcely suffered from lack of exercise. Records state that he was either ridden or driven on all his rounds.

The Johnson brothers kept Bulrush until 1837 when they sold him to the partnership of Blake and Foss in Chelsea, Vermont. He remained in their possession until 1842 and then at the ripe age of thirty he was sold to Lewis Jenkins of Fairlee, Vermont, and finally to F. A. Weir of Walpole, New Hampshire.

When he died at the remarkable age of thirty-six in 1848, Bulrush was as sound and clean-legged as any colt, and he had never been known to have a lame day in his very long life. All his family were just like him: tough and dependable, and with a dash of speed to satisfy the sport-minded.

THE THREE STUDS COMPARED

Linsley in a discourse on the similarities and differences between the Sherman, Woodbury and Bulrush families, wrote in 1857:

"Sherman had not so bold and resolute a style of action, and was not so nervous and high tempered as Woodbury; nor was he, in the language of the stable, so well 'finished up'; but he was more tractable, was exceedingly spirited, and a keen, rapid driver, possessed of great powers of endurance, a free and noble spirit, that needed neither whip nor spur, and courage that never flagged. . . . We think the Shermans are generally smaller than the Woodburys. They are more inclined to be hollow-backed, but their backs are very short, with wide, full and exceedingly muscular loins . . . none were known to have weak backs. . . . They have a shorter gait than the Bulrushes, and do not raise their feet as high. . . . They have not so bold, eager and commanding a style as the Woodburys, but we think they have a better temper for driving. They have a more rapid walk than either of the other families. . . . They are easily broken to harness. . . . The Shermans, like the Woodburys, are generally chestnut, being more common in this than the other families. A white stripe or star in the face and white hind feet are common. We think the Shermans have the best action in harness, and the Woodburys the best action under saddle.

"The founders of this the Woodbury family and of the Bulrush family were bred close together and remained near each other most of their lives; hence their descendants are found in the same vicinity [along the Connecticut River between Brattleboro and Newbury]. The average size of the Woodburys, we believe to be greater than either of the other families. They are deeper in the flanks with heavier quarters but not so heavy in the chest. Some are inclined to be hollow-backed and in this respect differ from the Bulrushes. They have an exceedingly bold, lofty and resolute style of action and are overflowing with spirit and nervous energy. They are generally very tractable but eager and restless; are full of ambition and cat-like activity and they make excellent parade horses. Their prevailing color is chestnut or bay with a white star or stripe in the face and white on one or both of the hind feet. Only a few of this family have long hair on the legs above the fetlocks and they do not generally have as heavy manes and tails as the other families. They have a shorter gait than the Bulrushes and are spirited and pleasant drivers. The limbs, with the exception that they are freer from long hairs, closely resemble the limbs of the Shermans, being not so large as the limbs of the Bulrushes. They have generally a softer coat than either of the other families. The Woodburys have the largest, most promi-

nent and brightest eyes of any of the Morgans. The forehead is also
very broad and the muzzle good, but in some of them the jowls are
not so well shaped as the others. . . .

"[The Bulrush family] are almost invariably deep bays and browns
with black legs, manes and tails; in this respect they differ from the
other families and also in their general freedom from any marks:
such as white feet or white spots in the face. They have large limbs,
wide, flat and muscular, sometimes inclined to be a little coarse, but
joints are good and the whole limbs very large in proportion to the
size of the animal. We do not recollect ever seeing a spavin or a ring-
bone on a Bulrush horse. They exhibit great development of muscle
and in point of size are fully equal to the average of Morgans. They
have not so bright, lively and intelligent eyes as the other families,
though the eyes are by no means dull or stupid. They do not carry
their heads as high, nor do they have as bold and eager an expression as the Woodburys or as graceful and easy motion as the Shermans, but for lastingness and power of endurance, we believe they

have no rivals in this or any other country among Morgans or any other breed. There is really some ground for the assertion once made that 'a smart, active boy would wear out a wrought-iron pony sooner than a grown man could break down the constitution of a Bulrush horse.' In addition to this power of endurance, they are generally sharp, keen drivers and many of them are fast. They are not excitable, never fret upon the road but are busy industrious workers. Some of the family have considerable long hair upon the legs and others are entirely free from it. Most of them have very heavy manes and tails."

The above was written when men were numerous who had known the horses spoken of and could give eyewitness accounts of the Morgans of those early days. While Linsley tends to repeat himself on a few occasions and comes a bit close even to contradicting himself, still his account of the Morgans at the time of their birth as a breed is the most thorough and detailed of anything that has ever been written about them.

REVENGE

The fourth of Justin Morgan's sons known to have been kept at stud was Revenge, whose history is far less complete than that of his famous brothers. He was a dark bay or light brown, foaled in Claremont, New Hampshire, in 1815, and was the property of Cyrus Moore of that town. His dam was a brown mare, marked with a white stripe and white hind socks. She was smart enough in harness, despite an inclination to be low-headed and an unattractive tendency to pace. No one seems to know anything about her sire, but her dam was thought to have a bit of Narragansett pacer blood in her veins, which would account for her daughter's gait.

Moore sold Revenge the autumn after he was two years old to Nehemiah Rice. Rice kept him two or three years, and then sold him to a Mr. Tyler who kept him in the vicinity of Claremont until the horse was nine years old. He had a number of owners after that. In April 1837 he had been driven to Chester, Vermont, by his current owner, who had intended to drive on to the western part of the state; but in Chester the horse became sick and died suddenly.

Revenge was about 14.2 hands high and weighed a substantial 1,000 pounds. He did not have an overabundance of action nor a very smooth gait, yet despite his mother's breeding he never paced or hitched. It was reported that he had plenty of get up and go and great endurance to boot, and was "hard to get away from on the road." He is reported, however, to have had one fault in harness. He had been frightened as a colt when a portion of his harness parted company with the buggy and he was known to have taken off. He never really recovered from the effects of this frightening experience, and would "take an awful hold" when driven singly and something spooked him.

His stock were dark bay or brown and sometimes chestnut. They had good size, were strong, hardy and enduring. They were generally free going in harness, although some of them would both pace and trot. None of his get approached the fame of his three notable brothers' offspring.

THE HAWKINS HORSE

The two other sons of Justin which Linsley was able to trace with accuracy were the Hawkins horse and the Fenton horse.

The Hawkins horse was foaled in 1806 or 1807, the property of a Mr. Melvin of St. Johnsbury, Vermont. His dam was a bay, standing about 15 hands, and with good conformation and excellent action. She was sired by a black horse brought from Connecticut and said to have been an imported Thoroughbred racer. When the colt was three years old, Melvin sold him to Olney Hawkins, a near neighbor. Hawkins was the captain of a troop, and bought the colt to use as a parade horse. He kept the horse five or six years and then sold him to his brother Stephen. Stephen stabled the stallion at St. Johnsbury for a period of two years and then took him to Stanstead, Quebec, not far over the border from St. Johnsbury. While in Stanstead the horse was bred to some of the local mares, and left some stock in the surrounding countryside. From that locality he was taken to northern Canada and all trace of him seems lost thereafter, for no record has been found of where he was kept or when he died.

The Hawkins horse was a jet black, about 15 hands, and not quite so compact as his sire, being a little taller and a bit heavier. His shoulders, back and loins were excellent. He carried his head high, had a bold, smart way of going, and was said to be the fastest of Justin's six known sons. He was a good trotter and extremely speedy at the gallop. His eye was a little fierce in its expression, and he was inclined to be cross and not so tractable as the rest; however he was one of the best-moving and finest-looking horses under saddle ever seen in Vermont.

THE FENTON HORSE

Richard Fenton of St. Johnsbury was the owner of Justin's sixth known son at stud, foaled in 1808. His dam was bay and of unknown blood. The only particulars known about her were that she was a familiar horse in the neighborhood and was supposedly an excellent individual.

The Fenton horse was a bright blood-bay with black points, and stood about 14.2 hands high. He was the image of old Justin: very compact and muscular. Linsley refers to him as being one of Justin's best sons, but fate had other plans for him than to sire a line of Morgans. He bit his owner (as some studs have a habit of doing at regular intervals) quite severely; the owner decided he would be happier with a gelding, thus ending the horse's potential as a sire.

III

Descendants of Sherman:

Black Hawk, Ethan Allen and Daniel Lambert

SHERMAN'S line comes down to us today in greater abundance than that of Justin's other sons not so much because he himself was superior to his brothers Woodbury and Bulrush, but because his siring of the famous racer Black Hawk put him into the public eye. Horsemen throughout New England, recognizing Black Hawk's greatness, sought out individuals which traced to Sherman's blood. Hoping for speedy, stylish colts, breeders looked to this line, and thus in retrospect the scales were tipped numerically in Sherman's favor.

BLACK HAWK

Probably the best-known son of old Sherman Morgan was the famous stallion Black Hawk. For many years he was the *beau idéal* of horsemen everywhere, and he founded a family which almost became a breed unto itself. His name was almost a household word, obscuring all others for nearly all his lifetime; meanwhile he established himself in his day as the head of the largest and most popular branch of old Justin Morgan's family.

That old Black Hawk was "bred in the purple" has been proved almost conclusively by students of the Morgan breed. Despite references which tend to disagree as to the origin of his dam, the majority state that she was of English or Thoroughbred blood, and that she first saw the light of day in Nova Scotia. All who knew her were quick to admit she was a fine animal and were always ready with

their praise of her. We must go along with their statements and conjure up our own picture of the dam of Black Hawk, however, for there has never been discovered any likeness of her in the old engravings although her son was the subject of many. At the time Black Hawk was foaled in the early spring of 1833, the black mare was the property of Ezekiel Twombly of Durham, New Hampshire. Previously she had been owned by Benjamin Kelly of Durham, who is said to have gotten her from a peddler; and goodness knows where the peddler had acquired her. Actually, except for the Nova Scotia story, nothing else really has much basis in fact.

In every way the dam of Black Hawk was supposedly a fine animal. She is described as being a large mare, standing about 16 hands; jet black in color, with a white stripe in her face being her only marking. She had a good head and she carried her ears alertly although they were a bit long. Her neck was a good length, her throat clean and cut up under the jowl. She had a strong back, good croup and quarters. Her legs were clean and "breedy looking" and free from long hair at the cannons.

In 1832 she came into the possession of Twombly in a horse-trading deal with Benjamin Kelly of Durham. The mare had been bred to Sherman Morgan early in the spring with the agreement that, should she prove safely in foal, Twombly owed Kelly a load of hay to seal the bargain!

The mare foaled right on schedule the following April, despite the fact that Kelly had used her extensively in harness and had even driven her a measured mile on the turnpike at a three-minute clip while she was in foal; Twombly had also driven her, after becoming her new owner, up until the time she foaled. All who knew her attested to the fact that she was a mare with unusual endurance and excellent wind. She was safe for anyone to drive and was comparatively alert and high-headed in harness. It is suggested by some authorities that she had a tendency to pace, but most sources indicate this to be unlikely. More mention is made of the fact that she was a fast trotter than that she would pace when urged. In short, throughout the vicinity of Durham she had the reputation of being an outstanding roadster.

The black mare remained in the possession of Twombly's family after his death, but in 1841 when the old lady became lame, Shadrack Seavey, a nephew of Twombly's who had acquired Black Hawk in the meantime, took over the selling of her for the family. She had had two colts by her son Black Hawk, but both of these died. As all record of her was lost after she was sent down the road, it is anybody's guess whether she ever had any others.

When he was foaled, Black Hawk was as unpromising a colt as one could imagine. He was downright homely, and the neighbors assured Twombly that he'd be lucky if he got a hundred dollars out of him, grown!

The care, and soon the training, of Black Hawk became the task of Twombly's aforementioned nephew, Shadrack Seavey. Later the colt was given to Seavey; he was the first one to bridle him and train him to harness and saddle. When Twombly died in 1837 his property was appraised to include the value of the colt Black Hawk as $60. This sum Seavey paid to become the legal owner.

Black Hawk was always a square trotter from the very beginning, never showing any inclination to pace. He was amazingly intelligent and good-natured. Not once is it recorded that he offered to kick or run off even though the old harness would break repeatedly during his training. All the while Seavey owned him, Black Hawk was never passed on the road, and so strong was his trotting gait that he was never known to break no matter how tightly pressed. As well as being fast, Black Hawk had belied his early appearance by developing into an exceedingly handsome horse. In many ways he resembled his dam, especially through the head.

When he was two years old, the young rascal escaped his pasture on several occasions—and his first foals arrived the following year! Such a nuisance was this, and so annoyed were the neighbors by the clatter of hoofs in the night, that Seavey decided to have the young stallion gelded. But when the deed was arranged for and about to be carried out, the man who was to perform the operation strongly urged Seavey to change his mind, stating that the horse was far too good an animal to geld. The loss to the Morgan breed had this operation been performed would have been of such magnitude as almost to have doomed the breed. Luckily Seavey saw the light, as it were, and agreed that perhaps the stud was worth considering again.

Seavey kept Black Hawk until the horse was a five-year-old and then he traded him for a mare and $50 to A. R. Mathes, who reportedly lived in Connecticut. We wonder why he should have been

Black Hawk and Lady Suffolk.

so foolish as to let the good horse go, but can only surmise that perhaps he preferred a mare to the unpredictable ways of a young stallion. At any rate, who's ever to try to explain just exactly what motivates any horse-trading deal? Seavey made his trade and Mathes gained one of the best Morgan stallions ever to look through a bridle. However it seems that Mathes was, although an astute horseman, perhaps slightly more interested in the almighty dollar than in the ownership of a promising stallion; for after only a short time —approximately five weeks—he sold Black Hawk for $200, a sizable return on his original investment.

Black Hawk's new owners, Messrs. Brown and Thurston of Haverhill, Massachusetts, were interested primarily in the trotting speed of their new horse (which had increased noticeably even in the short time Mathes had owned him). Brown sold out his interest in Black Hawk to Thurston, however, after a short time. It was Thurston who gave the stud the name Black Hawk (he is known today as Black Hawk 20, in accordance with his registration number later assigned to him in Volume III of the *Register*).

At maturity this black son of Sherman was as handsome a horse as could be found anywhere. He stood 15 hands and weighed around 1,000 pounds. His finely chiseled head bespoke quality in every line. His eyes were large and very bright; his nostrils would flare to a size to hold a man's fist when distended. He had a short, strong back, being close-ribbed and compact. His shoulders were deep and well sloped, and his muscling was superb throughout. He was a symmetrical horse from all angles, each part blending into the other in the smoothest possible way. That such a horse as Black Hawk should have founded a fine line of Morgan horses is perfectly within the realm of understanding, for it is not from cold-blooded stock that equine stars find their beginnings.

Thurston, who was the first to bring Black Hawk out on the trotting courses, used the horse for six years as a family horse. He stated that Black Hawk was the finest horse he had ever owned in the considerable number which had come his way. He praised him as an excellent roadster, saying that no matter how far or fast he traveled the stallion never showed any signs of fatigue. He praised his disposition as second to none, either for himself or any other member of his family, and he stated that the stock of Black Hawk were like their sire in all respects.

Thurston was known to have driven the horse in many trotting contests of the day, and so far as records show he was never beaten. The records may be few, but they show that in Boston in 1842 he

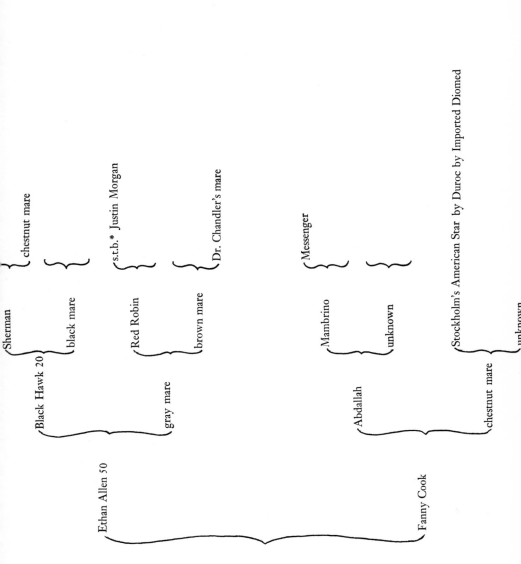

- Daniel Lambert
  - Ethan Allen 50
    - Black Hawk 20
      - Sherman
        - chestnut mare
      - black mare
    - gray mare
      - Red Robin
        - s.t.b.* Justin Morgan
      - brown mare
        - Dr. Chandler's mare
  - Fanny Cook
    - Abdallah
      - Mambrino
        - Messenger
      - unknown
    - chestnut mare
      - Stockholm's American Star by Duroc by Imported Diomed
      - unknown

*said to be

won a race of five miles in sixteen minutes for a purse of $1,000; a year later, at the age of ten, he won in straight heats a best-three-in-five race of two-mile heats for $400. His best time for the two miles was 5:43. His record for the mile was 2:42, a time he made on numerous occasions.

Black Hawk was not used at stud to any great degree until he came into the ownership of David Hill of Bridport, Vermont, in 1844. After the arrival of his first foals, however, his service became very much in demand. Mares from all over New England and New York, as well as some Canadian provinces, were brought to him. The fee he commanded was $100, the highest figure paid for stud service at that time.

His greatest son, of course, was Ethan Allen 50, whose virtues we shall extol farther along. But other foals with lesser reputation sold for between $1,000 and $3,000, with some prices even higher. His stud earnings exceeded $34,000. No record indicates that any of his offspring were inferior or did not command good prices.

Where or when he died has never been recorded, so far as I've been able to discover. It is strange and sad that a horse so venerated should have no monument, even a verbal one. However because he was so valued he certainly must have spent his last days in comfort.

In Black Hawk's day, road horses and race horses were much in demand, and the influence of this famous stallion easily can be seen by tracing back the pedigrees of many well-known Standardbred horses. His influence on other breeds is also quite clearly apparent. Billy Direct, the Standardbred who held the world's record for the mile (1:55) traces to Black Hawk. A Black Hawk-line mare produced George Wilkes, one of the greatest trotting sires of all time. And his influence on the American Saddlebred horse can be traced through such offspring as his son BLOOD's BLACK HAWK and his grandson INDIAN CHIEF. Bourbon King and the great Edna May's King come from Black Hawk blood.

Few Morgans of modern times do not trace back to old Black Hawk in countless lines. Indeed, as high a figure as 80 percent go back through his sons to this prolific black grandson of Justin.

BILLY ROOT (*also called Comet*), *from Linsley.*

BILLY ROOT

A small, compact horse with a deep, cresty neck and a sprightly countenance was Billy Root. He would scarcely tip the scales by more than 950 pounds or stand more than 14 hands, but every atom of him was bubbling with personality and vigor. His back was round and short, with the smooth compactness of his sire and grandsire. In color he was a very dark chestnut, with a faint star and a bit of white on his off hind pastern. His legs and feet were exceptionally good, a trait noted in his offspring; no lameness was ever discovered.

Although he resembled his sire, Sherman, very closely, Billy Root had a personality all his own. He was quite mischievous in a playful way and delighted in making off with any blanket or strap left casually hanging over a fence or gate. Chasing hens or sheep were to Billy a sport to be indulged in whenever possible—undoubtedly to the complete chagrin of his owners. His antics, however, probably could be overlooked, because Billy Root was as willing a worker as his sire and old Justin had been.

In his lifetime he knew many owners and traveled extensively throughout New England, leaving behind progeny which were celebrated for their spirit, action, endurance and docility.

Billy's dam was said to be half French (Canadian) and sired by Justin Morgan. She was a fine road horse with undoubtedly amazing endurance, for she was said to have been driven the 120 miles between St. Johnsbury, Vermont, and Portland, Maine, in one day on at least three occasions! Little Billy was her only known foal: long before his value was realized, she had been sold down into southern Vermont, and all trace of her was lost.

Billy Root was foaled in St. Johnsbury in 1829, the property of a man by the name of Hezekiah Morton. Early in his life he was known as Red Bird, but acquired the name Comet when purchased by Eldad Root in 1832 or '33. From St. Johnsbury he was taken by Root to the Genessee Valley in New York State. There he stood at stud for several seasons before returning to Vermont a few years later. His travels were quite extensive after that, and he made stud seasons in Lyndonville and Highgate in Vermont, where he remained four years. It was during this period that Root parted with the little stallion. His next owner's name was Stephens, and it was he who began calling the horse Billy Root.

But Billy didn't stay long with Stephens. Despite his being by then about twelve years old, he spent the next few years in the service of many owners in different parts of New England. He always was remembered in the different localities by the fine, strong colts with bright eyes and cheery dispositions; colts which, like their sire, would rather prance than walk and which, although small, were always ready and willing to tackle any load no matter how heavy.

In 1847 when the stallion was eighteen, the local farmers around the vicinity of Lyndon and Highgate requested that Billy be brought back to Vermont. And there he remained through the seasons of 1847 through 1851. Then in April 1852 little Billy's unexpected death shocked the horsemen for miles around. It was said that his death was caused by the rupture of a blood vessel.

Billy Root was always noted for the quality of his daughters as well as of his sons. His name comes down to us in many modern pedigrees, while he himself will always be remembered as the personification of the old-time Morgan horse.

ETHAN ALLEN

Probably of all the now-legendary names within the Morgan breed during the nineteenth century, none can surpass the great Ethan

ETHAN ALLEN 50

Allen 50. This best-known son of the celebrated Black Hawk was perhaps the most famous horse of his day, and it certainly could be said safely that he even outranked his venerable sire in popularity, as well as overshadowing his second cousin, the widely shown HALE'S GREEN MOUNTAIN. For Ethan Allen's name also became almost a household word during his illustrious career—he was the epitome of America's ideal horse, a perfect horse in about every sense of the word: there was no finer example of beauty and symmetry, coupled with lightning speed at the trot, than could be seen in the form of this one Morgan stallion.

His fame extended from ocean to ocean, so publicized were his achievements. It is no overstatement to say that he was the darling of the racing public, and sports writers were hard put to keep from running out of superlatives to describe him. Win or lose, his style and speed were everywhere acclaimed. Cheers followed his every race; whether he was first under the wire or not, it made little difference. At four years of age, with a mark of 2:25½, he was named Champion of the World, and his phenomenal mark of 2:15, when matched against the might Dexter, topped a long list of honors in the trotting world. This famous race will be described shortly.

Just the appearance of Ethan Allen on any racecourse triggered the wildest applause, for even the most callous racegoer could not fail to be affected by his well-rounded Morgan conformation—which even in racing condition gave him the smoothness and symmetry for which Morgans were famous, then as well as now. His excellent disposition also made him a great favorite with his many owners and the men who worked with him.

S. W. Parlin, writing in the contemporary *American Cultivator,* describes Ethan Allen as follows:

"No one ever raised a doubt as to his being the handsomest and most perfectly gaited trotter that has ever been produced. Horsemen will agree that no trotter has ever appeared upon the turf that excelled him in the style and beauty of his action, whether moving at a jog or flying at the rate of a mile in 2:15. His trotting instinct was wonderfully strong and his disposition the best imaginable, two qualities which enabled him when hitched with a running mate, to outstrip every competitor that could be brought against him in that rig. During the season of 1861, hitched with a runner, he won three races from the world-renowned Flora Temple, rigged in the same style, in one of which he placed his mark at 2:19¾. In May, 1867, at the Union Course, Long Island, he beat Brown George and running mate in straight heats, time: 2:29, 2:21, 2:19. The crowning event of his life, however, was the race in which, hitched with running mate, he challenged the admiration of the world by defeating the great Dexter, which was then supposed to be invincible, at the Fashion Course, June 21, 1867, in short order, landing at the wire in 2:15, 2:16 and 2:19 respectively. Good judges estimated him capable of trotting the first heat in 2:12 had he been sent with that intention."

Ethan Allen 50 was foaled in Ticonderoga, New York, on June 18, 1849, and was raised, it is said, as a family pet. His owner was Joel W. Holcomb, who had acquired the colt's dam in the fall of 1844. She was a mouse-gray mare, foaled in 1830 and owned at the time by John Field of Springfield, Vermont. She was said to be by a small bay horse known as Red Robin, who was bred down on the Connecticut River at Weathersfield Bow at a time when Justin Morgan himself stood just across the bridge in Claremont, New Hampshire. Many authorities are quite convinced that Red Robin was by old Justin because of his marked degree of resemblance to the original Morgan.

Ethan Allen's second dam was a brown mare who also resembled the early Morgans, and according to local records was quite possibly out of a daughter of Justin. These opinions, if proved for a certainty, would give Ethan Allen a very strong percentage of the blood of Justin Morgan.

Volume I of the *American Morgan Horse Register* states, pertaining to Red Robin:

"We have given the substance of all evidence which we have been able to get relative to the history of Red Robin. It is probable that he was foaled in 1816 and that he came into the hands of Moses Bates before 1820. . . . At best, his breeder and breeding are purely a matter of conjecture, but the opinion of Mr. Bisbee, who knew him [Red Robin] well, that he was by the Justin Morgan, is very probably correct. It certainly is sustained by the character and appearance of the horse and by the fact that the original Morgan horse stood near where he was begotten and not improbably included in

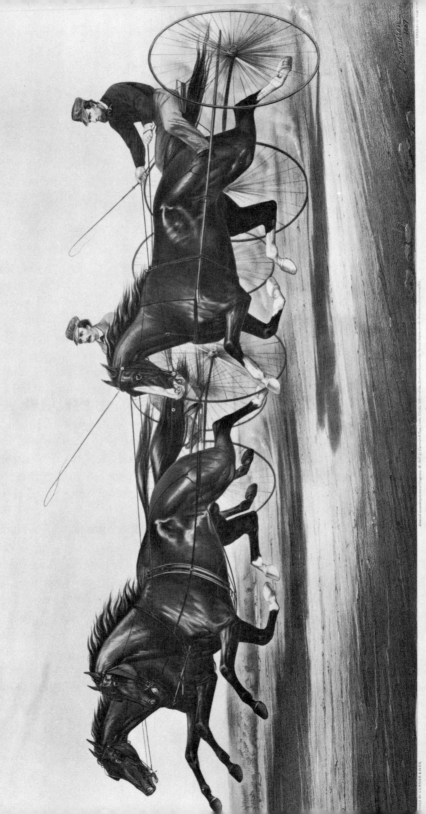

ETHAN ALLEN AND MATE AND DEXTER.

his circuit the town of Springfield itself in 1815, the year that Robin is supposed to have been bred."

The dam of Ethan Allen was used at regular farm labor until she was four years old. She was a willing worker despite a lack of size, and was a good mare on the road as well, being intelligent and docile in harness. At four she was sold to F. A. Leland, who put her to a peddler's wagon. She was driven along a route in New York State in the vicinity of Hague, Schroon and Whitehall. Because she was likely to be nervous and frightened whenever goods were taken from the wagon, she was traded to Rufus Rising of Hague for a gray gelding. Subsequently she was returned to heavy farm work, the result of which was a bad spavin, and was retired to the rank of brood mare in 1841. She produced three excellent colts from 1842 to 1844 and finally, in the fall of '44, became the property of Joel Holcomb. Previous to foaling the great Ethan Allen in 1849 (who proved to be her last offspring), this fine old mare produced a top mare of her day, BLACK HAWK MAID (2:37), by Black Hawk, as well as three other outstanding colts. She had foaled regularly for eight consecutive years and died in foal, again to Black Hawk, in 1851 at the age of twenty-one.

Ethan Allen 50 (his number, too, was assigned him in Volume III) was a remarkable colt even at an early age. That he truly was a family pet is proved by Mrs. Holcomb, who reportedly said, "You couldn't get him by the window but that he would put his head in to get a piece of cake." His beautiful conformation and kindly ways made him loved and admired by all who knew him even in those early days.

Ethan was a bright bay in color, with a small star and faint snip between his nostrils. He was liberally marked with white, having, besides the star and snip, three socks as well. At maturity he stood slightly under 15 hands and weighed 1,000 pounds in top condition. For a stallion, his head was remarkably fine, with large, bright and expressive eyes; sharply defined, small ears, and a full, flowing forelock to lend effect. His neck, with its clean-cut throttle, was of good length and not too heavily crested, blending smoothly into deep, oblique shoulders with well-defined withers. He had an excellent level back, with powerfully muscled croup and quarters. Despite his deep shoulders and long hipline—which gave him the look of being a bit long for his height—Ethan Allen was very symmetrical. With his lovely head carried high he was without a doubt one of the most beautiful of horses. His long flowing black mane and tail completed the picture.

Holcomb sold a half-interest in Ethan Allen to Orville S. Roe of Shoreham, Vermont, when the animal was still a colt, and during the earliest years of his life he was owned jointly by them both. The stallion was used for stud service both at Shoreham and also for a number of seasons at Cambridge, Massachusetts. Ethan Allen's greatest sons were sired during his seasons at Shoreham. Among them were DANIEL LAMBERT, AMERICAN ETHAN, HOLABIRD'S ETHAN ALLEN, DeLONG'S ETHAN ALLEN and HONEST ALLEN. Through Honest Allen his male line is carried down to us through DENNING ALLEN, the sire of GENERAL GATES, who in turn became the foundation sire of the United States Morgan Horse Farm near Middlebury, Vermont.

During this same period Ethan was also put to racing nearly every season, and even in those early days he won most of his many contests.

As a Sire

From 1862, when he was sold to Frank Baker, Ethan Allen knew many owners and traveled many miles for both racing and stud service. His fame grew, and the demand for his services increased with his prestige. In 1869 at Medford, Massachusetts, his fee was $100. In 1870 at the same location it was raised to $200 the season.

Ethan Allen sired over seventy winners of the trotting world, among them six sons which were listed as standard trotters; of them, BILLY BARR (2:23¾) and HOTSPUR (2:24) were the fastest. He also sired FANNY ALLEN, a bay mare with a mark of 2:28¼, and another bay mare, POCAHONTAS (2:26¾), for whom Robert Bonner paid the phenomenal price of $40,000. This mare was also a great roadster and had an unofficial record of 2:17¾ when driven by her owner on the road. That she never produced a foal was a fact Bonner much regretted.

Probably the best known of Ethan Allen's sons was Daniel Lambert, a sire in his own right of speedy trotters and snappy-going road horses. More about this stallion and his influence on trotting-bred and saddle-bred horses will follow this chapter.

Despite the fact that he was not unbeaten on the race track, Ethan Allen was the high-lighted personality of every race he entered. His well-balanced, brilliant action has been portrayed without exaggeration in many prints by Currier and Ives. He also reigns supreme over many a New England barn, as innumerable weather vanes carry his likeness. He was a point of comparison: if someone noted that a horse resembled old Ethan Allen, he was paying the animal the highest compliment. Even in later years when the lean, long-limbed (and homely!) Messengers and Hambletonians had taken over the racing scene and all Ethan Allen's records had fallen, old-timers still talked of the great Ethan Allen, and the Morgan beauty he brought to the race track.

The Race with Dexter

Ethan's greatest race, and the one which assured his permanent niche in the Racing Hall of Fame, was the famous match against the champion trotter of the day, Dexter (2:19), a son of Rysdyk's Hambletonian.

This race is said to have been witnessed by an estimated forty thousand people. The following long passage by John H. Wallace, editor at the time of the *American Trotting Register* and an actual eyewitness, undoubtedly gives the most vivid description of Ethan Allen's greatest victory. Remembering that Ethan was at this time eighteen years of age and a veteran of many seasons at stud, as well as having been a participant in countless matches against the best trotters of his day, gives added impact to his victory. Here is Wallace's account as published in *Wallace's Monthly* of April 1877 (note that it was accepted procedure to hitch a mate to the light racing vehicle to set the pace by galloping alongside; a strange practice to our modern notions, and possibly the origin of the political expression "running mate"):

On the 21st of June 1867, on the Fashion Course, it was my good fortune to witness the crowning event of his [Ethan's] life. Some three weeks before, Ethan, with a running mate, had beaten Brown George and running mate in very fast time, scoring one heat in 2:19. This made horsemen open their eyes and there at once arose a difference of opinion about the advantage to the trotter of having a runner hitched with him to pull the weight. This resulted in a match for twenty-five hundred dol-

Detail from Ethan's race with George M. Patchen.

lars a side, to trot Ethan and running mate against Dexter, who was then considered invincible. As the day approached, the betting was about even; but the evening before the race, word came from the course that Ethan's running mate had fallen lame and could not go, but they would try to get Brown George's running mate, then in Connecticut, to take the place of the lame runner. As the horses were strangers to each other, it was justly concluded, the change gave Dexter a great advantage and the betting at once changed from even to two to one on Dexter. Long before noon the crowd began to assemble and sporting men everywhere were shaking rolls of green backs over their heads, shouting, "Two to one on Dexter." I met a friend from Chicago, who sometimes speculates a little and when he told me he was betting "two to one on Dexter," I took the liberty of advising him to be cautious, for I thought the team would win the race and that its backers knew what they were doing. Before the hour arrived, I secured a seat on the ladies' stand, from which every foot of the course and the countless multitude of people could be taken in at a glance. The vehicles were simply incalculable and the people were like a vast sea. The multitude was estimated at forty thousand!

Upon the arrival of the hour, the judges ascended the stand and rang up the horses, when the backers of the team came forward, explained the mishap that had befallen the runner, that they had Brown George's mate on the grounds, but, as he and Ethan had never been hitched together, they were unwilling to risk so large a sum and closed the race by paying one thousand, two hundred and fifty dollars forfeit. When this announcement was made, there was a general murmur that spread, step by step, through all the vast multitude. The betting fraternity were just where they started and every spectator realized a feeling of disgust at the whole management. As soon as this had had time to exert its intended effect upon the crowd, the backers of the team came forward again and, expressing their unwillingness to have the people go away dissatisfied, proposed a little match of two hundred and fifty dollars a side, which was promptly accepted by the Dexter party; and when it was known that there would be a race after all, the shout of the multitude was like the voice of many waters. This being a new race, the betting men had to commence again. The surroundings of the pool stands were packed with an eager and excited crowd, anxious to get on their money at two, and, rather than miss, at three to one on Dexter. The work of the auctioneers was "short, sharp and decisive," and the tickets were away up in the hundreds and oftentimes in the thousands. But the pool stands did not seem to accommodate more than a small fraction of those anxious to invest and in all directions, in the surging crowd, hands were in the air, filled with rolls of greenbacks and shouting, "Two to one on Dexter!" I was curious to note what became of these noisy offers and I soon observed that a quiet-looking man came along, took all one party had to invest and then quietly went to another of the shouters, and then another, and so on, till I think everyone who had money to invest at that rate was accommodated. The amount of money bet was enormous, no doubt aggregating a quarter of a million in a few minutes.

When the horses appeared upon the track to warm up for the race, Dexter, driven by the accomplished reinsman, Budd Doble, was greeted with a shout of applause. Soon the team appeared and behind it sat the great master of trotting tactics, Dan Mace. His face, which has so often been a puzzle to thousands, had no mask over it on this occasion. It spoke only that intense earnestness that indicates the near approach of a supreme moment. The team was hitched to a light skeleton wagon; Ethan wore breeching and beside him was a great, strong race-horse, fit to run for a man's life. His traces were long enough to fully extend himself, but they were so much shorter than Ethan's that he had to take the weight. Dexter drew the inside and on the first trial they got the "send-off" without either one having six inches the advantage. When they got the word, the flight of speed was absolutely terrific, so far beyond anything I had ever witnessed in a trotting horse that I felt the hair rising on my head. The running horse was next to me and, not withstanding my elevation, Ethan was stretched out so near the ground that I could see nothing of him but his ears. I fully believe that for several rods at this point they were going at a two minute gait.

It was impossible that this terrible pace could be maintained long and just before reaching the first turn, Dexter's head began to swim and the team passed him and took the track, reaching the first quarter pole in thirty-two seconds, with Dexter three or four lengths behind. The same lightning speed was kept up through the second quarter, reaching the half-mile pole in 1:04, with Dexter still farther in the rear. Mace then took a pull on his team and came home a winner by six or eight lengths, in 2:15. When this time was put on the blackboard, the response of the multitude was like the roar of old ocean. Although some distance away, through the second quarter of this heat, I had a fair, unobstructed side-view of the stallion and of his action, when going at the lightning rate of 2:08 to the mile. I could not observe that he received the slightest degree of propulsion from the running horse; and my conviction was then, and is now that any such propulsion would have interfered with his own unapproachable action and would have retarded, rather than helped him. The most noticeable feature in his style of movement was the remarkable lowness to which he dropped his body and the straight gliding line it maintained at that elevation.

The team now had the inside and in the first attempt they were started for the second heat. Before they had gone many rods Ethan lost his stride and Dexter took the track at the very spot where he had lost it in the first heat. The team soon got to work and near the beginning of the second quarter, collared Dexter, but the stallion broke soon after and fell back, not yards nor lengths but rods, before he caught. Incredible as it may seem, when he again got his feet he put on such a burst of speed as to overhaul the flying Dexter in the third quarter, when he broke again and Mace had to pull him nearly to a standstill before he recovered. Dexter was now a full distance ahead and the heat appeared to be his beyond all peradventure. I was watching the team in its troubles very closely and my idea of the distance lost was the result of a deliberate and careful estimate at the moment; and the query in my mind then was, whether the team could save its distance. At last the old horse struck his gait and it was like a dart from a catapult, or a ball from a rifle. The team not only saved its distance, but beat Dexter home, five or six lengths, in 2:16.

In the third heat Mace had it all his own way throughout, coming home the winner of the race in 2:19. The backers of Dexter, up to the very last, placed great reliance on his well-known staying qualities; but the last heat showed that the terrible struggle had told upon him more distressingly than on the team. It is said by those who timed Dexter privately that he trotted the three heats in 2:17, 2:18, 2:21.

If ever there was an honest race trotted, this was one, but there was such a specimen of sharp diplomacy, of "diamond cut diamond," in the preliminaries, as is seldom witnessed, even on a race course. It is not probable that Ethan's intended running mate fell amiss at all, the evening before, as represented; and if she did, it was not possible to send to Connecticut for another horse and have him there early the morning of the race, as was pretended. This was a mere ruse put out to get the advantage of the long odds. The backers of the team knew just how the horses would work and knew they had speed enough to beat any horse on earth. When the race was called and they came forward and paid forfeit, it was merely to give the "two-to-one-on Dexter" money encouragement to come out. It did come out most vociferously and was all quietly taken. It was said John Morrissey was the manager-in-chief and that his share of the winnings amounted to about forty thousand dollars.

After witnessing the second heat and studying it carefully, I am firmly of the opinion the team could have gone the first heat in 2:12 if it had been necessary.

Monument in Kansas

On October 17, 1870, old Ethan Allen was sold for the last time. His newest owner was Colonel Amasa Sprague of Providence, Rhode Island. The price reportedly paid for this famous stallion was $7,500. Ethan was kept in Providence for a time before being sent by his owner to the Sprague and Akers Stock Farm at Lawrence, Kansas. Here the venerable old campaigner and idol of millions spent his last years in peace and contentment, far from the noisy race tracks and their cheering throngs. At last, on the 10th of September, 1876, in the twenty-eighth year of his life, old Ethan Allen died. He was buried at the entrance of the Trotting Park in Lawrence, where a monument was erected to his memory.

Thus passed one of the Morgan breed's brightest stars. But his greatness lives on down through the years in the breeding line of countless modern Morgans. Breeders today still point with pride to the crosses to Ethan Allen 50 in their horses' pedigrees, for even now his blood means a trace of beauty from the past.

DANIEL LAMBERT

During his lifetime Daniel Lambert, the son of great-hearted Ethan Allen 50, was applauded and acclaimed for many things, but possibly his major contribution to the Morgan fame was the siring of so many superior roadsters. The scores of sons and daughters of this prominent stallion, with their stylish mien and trotting speed on the road, gave their sire the vote of all New England horsemen as one of the greatest progenitors of trotters that ever stood in the Northeast. Even though the majority of his offspring never saw a race track, it is said that "they could beat a 2:30 horse down the road with ease." And their elegance and spirit in harness were admired by anyone with a hankering for an outstanding horse.

The Lamberts were pure, open-gaited trotters, needing neither boots or weights; and, like all the Morgans, were willing and cheerful in disposition. Many a chance brush on the road left the competition eating dust when a Lambert horse struck his gait.

The age of the fast road horse has passed now, with its throbbing of trotters' hoofs gone from the open lanes, but there was a time when the ownership of a Lambert Morgan was equivalent to the possession of the snappiest, low-slung, roaring sports car made today. The folks by the general store in town were just as impressed when you drove down the dusty main street behind a sleek, smooth-gaited Morgan as the fellows by the drug store are nowadays when you pull up to the curb in your purring, chrome-trimmed, high-priced product of Detroit or Europe.

Time passes, progress changes our way of life, but I sometimes

DANIEL LAMBERT

wonder which would give the greater thrill: holding the lines on a speedy Lambert colt when he overtakes a friend on the road and, to the music of flashing hoofs, leaves the other behind in a burst of speed born of heart and sinew—or sitting at the wheel of a roaring, ground-skimming sports car as its tires squeal out each turn in the road and the landscape blurs in the corners of your eyes. For me there could be but one choice. . . .

Foaled in 1858, the son of Ethan Allen and a fiery, bright red chestnut mare named Fanny Cook, Daniel Lambert was bred and owned by William H. Cook of Ticonderoga, New York. His dam was by Abdallah, a good son of Mambrino, who himself was by Messenger, the founding father of the Standardbred horse. His second dam was by Stockholm's American Star, by Duroc, the best son of Imported Diomed. Since Mambrino traces back to the Darley Arabian and the Byerly Turk, some of the same blood that is said to have produced Justin Morgan flowed in the veins of Fanny Cook.

The mettlesome Fanny Cook inherited her nervousness from her sire, who was so high-strung that he was never broken to harness, and was a decided departure from the usual farm mares that dot the distaff side of early Morgan pedigrees. Bred by Montfort Van Kleek of Dutchess County, New York, she was said to be an extremely fast mare at the trot and the gallop, although quite likely she was difficult to handle due to her peppery disposition.

His Qualities

Even as a foal Daniel Lambert had the fineness and quality which was later to dazzle horsemen everywhere, and he was sold at four months to John Porter of Ticonderoga for $300. Since weanlings of that day and age generally sold for about $50, the colt was considered high-priced; but when, at the age of five, this same young stallion was sold by Porter for $3,000 to R. S. Denny of Boston, the original outlay seems insignificant.

Denny took the horse—known up until that time as the "Porter colt"—to Watertown, Massachusetts. Denny renamed the stallion Hippomenes, and took him to Saratoga, New York, as his roadster; and there the horse became the king of the road even in that famous mecca of fine horses.

When owned by Denny at Watertown, Daniel Lambert was not used at stud too frequently and so did not leave many offspring in Massachusetts. It would appear that he was used for the most part as Denny's own road horse, for the man would not permit him to be raced on the track, even though as a three-year-old colt Daniel Lambert had been driven to a mark of 2:42 by Dan Mace, the reinsman who had handled the lines on old Ethan Allen in the classic match against Dexter. At the time, Mace was so confident in the abilities of the untrained colt that he offered to trot him against any three-year-

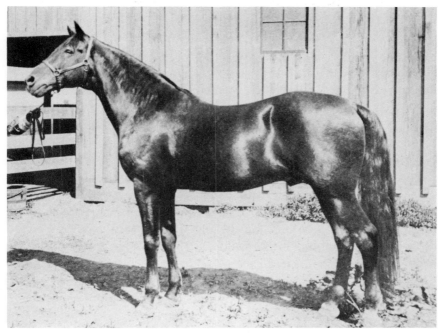

BEN FRANKLIN *by Daniel Lambert.*

old in the world for $5,000 or $10,000 a side. But, undoubtedly, knowing Mace and his keen knowledge of horseflesh, no one quite dared match a horse against him.

In harness Daniel Lambert's manners were as flawless as his gait, for he had inherited none of his dam's nervousness. He was never put into competition on the race track, but was shown as a driving horse at the fairs. The classes, and the only ones for harness exhibition at that time, were judged on a basis of one third for speed at the trot, one third for appearance and presence, i.e., showiness, and one third for manners. Needless to say, the golden beauty and matchless action of Daniel Lambert could not be bettered, and he was unbeaten in harness classes even when shown after his twentieth year.

As the horse was not having the opportunity of being used often at the stud in Watertown, Denny sold Daniel Lambert to Benjamin Bates when the stallion was eight years old. He made his first season at stud at the Cream Hill Stock Farm at Shoreham, Vermont, in 1866.

Each year for his next eleven years at Shoreham, Daniel Lambert was booked to an increasing number of mares. He remained at the Cream Hill Farm until 1877, when, upon Bates's death, he was removed to the Bates Farm back in Watertown, Massachusetts. He was sold to David Snow of Andover in 1880; later, in 1884, he was sold again to a company in Middlebury, Vermont, where he was stabled at the Bread Loaf Stock Farm, which was the property of Colonel Joseph A. Battell. There, enjoying a life of excellent health and vigor, and without a blemish or unsoundness, he remained until his death in 1889 at the age of thirty-one.

As with so many of the Morgans, age never seemed to fade the beauty of Daniel Lambert, and he remained a very handsome horse throughout his long life. He followed the Morgan pattern, too: he had a fine head, prominent eyes set wide apart, and short, alert ears; his clean-cut throttle, beautifully arched neck, deep shoulders, strong back, round barrel, broad, well-muscled loin and high-set tail were typical of his breeding. He had a lofty carriage, as do all true Morgans, and his bright chestnut coat, inherited from his dam, was fine and silky even in the winter months. His mane and tail were long and flaxen in color; he was marked with a narrow, even strip on his face, and a left hind sock. His forearms were long, broad and muscular; cannons short, with the bone being in good proportion to weight of body. He had excellent feet—a trait which he readily passed on to his offspring.

Colonel Battell in his Volume I of the Morgan *Register* quotes S. W. Parlin of Boston, who knew Daniel Lambert—and whose unreserved admiration for Ethan Allen has been noted—thus:

"By common consent the Morgans have enjoyed the reputation of being the most beautiful horses, as a family, ever produced on this continent and Lambert, when in his prime, was one of the most beautiful of that family. Few horses have ever lived that possessed greater power of stamping their offspring with the above characteristics and imparting the ability to perpetuate them through succeeding generations."

Lambert's Offspring

It was to the Green Mountain State that Daniel Lambert left his greatest heritage, for during his two stays in Vermont he was bred to some 1,100 mares. Although few of his colts were developed or trained for the track, as mentioned earlier, 106 of them were winners of 465 races, 37 of these having marks within the 2:30 standard.

Without exception Daniel Lambert's get were pure trotters. They ranged in size from 14.3 to 15.3, with a few measuring larger. All possessed the spirit, beauty and tremendous stride of their sire.

One of his best sons was JUBILEE LAMBERT, who was out of a granddaughter of old Black Hawk. He was bred by John Porter, who had owned Lambert till the stallion was five years old. Jubilee Lambert was a 15.3-hand bay foaled in 1863, and most of his life was spent in the vicinity of Cynthiana, Kentucky, where he was known for siring colts with outstanding show ability and presence. JUBILEE DE JARNETTE—out of the great show mare, LADY DE JARNETTE, by Indian Chief, a grandson of Black Hawk—was by Jubilee Lambert, and was considered his finest son.

Through the blood of Jubilee Lambert the early American Saddlebred gained much of its beauty and ability. Some of the greatest names in that breed trace back to Morgan through the sons and daughters of Jubilee Lambert.

IV

Descendants of Woodbury:

Gifford and Hale's Green Mountain Morgan

O F the three sons of Justin Morgan, undoubtedly Woodbury would enjoy the liveliest patronage were all three living to-day. With all the interest in the show ring now, breeders are striving to produce Morgans which exhibit an inborn showiness and an abundance of natural action. And Woodbury would be their ideal, for he certainly possessed all the symmetry, the bold eagerness and commanding style of action desired in today's show Morgans. Even in his own time Woodbury and his get were greatly admired for their style and beauty.

Although many of Woodbury's progeny were noted for the same beauty and performance of their sire, the fact should not be over-looked that speed, too, was inherent in Woodbury's line. He was the first horse foaled to leave three sons who each sired a 2:30 trotter: MORGAN CAESAR sired MAC (2:28) a 15.2-hand brown gelding foaled in 1848; MORGAN EAGLE sired LADY SUTTON (2:30), a fast brown mare who defeated the top mares of their day, Lady Suffolk and Lady Moscow; GIFFORD sired BEPPO (2:28), a good chestnut gelding who also gained fame as a racing crack.

The *American Morgan Horse Register* in reference to Woodbury's siring of speed horses notes that "early were the grandchildren of Woodbury Morgan from three different sons engaging in brilliant and successful trotting contests with the fastest and gamest in the land. Two of these three famous sons were founders of trotting families. A son of Morgan Eagle, bearing the same name, got MAGNA

CHARTA (2:33), that at one time held the four-year-old trotting record of the world, and became one of the foremost among the trotting sires in Michigan."

According to Linsley, Woodbury sired eighteen sons which became outstanding sires in their own right. Of these, chestnut seems to have been the prevailing color and the average height was 15 hands and weight 1,050. Besides the above-mentioned stallions, the BABBITT HORSE, the PUTNAM HORSE, GENERAL HIBBARD and the NICHOLS HORSE were popular studs in their day.

GIFFORD MORGAN

As a model for old Justin, GIFFORD MORGAN, too, could qualify almost without a change except for color. And all his stock were also very much like the get of the old horse.

Gifford was a small, dark chestnut replica of his grandsire, and the smallest of Woodbury's sons. He resembled little Billy Root in build, being pony-sized and short-legged. But despite his size Gifford's action and style and his spirited outlook were unexcelled by other horses of his time.

Gifford was foaled in Tunbridge, Vermont, on June 13, 1824, the property of Ziba Gifford of that town. His dam, a bright bay with a great deal of quality, was sired by Henry Dundas, who was by Woolsey, a large bay who was one of the first Thoroughbreds of proved ancestry in New England. There was no doubt as to the fact that Gifford's dam was a high-bred mare tracing to some of the best of the early imported Thoroughbreds; yet persons who knew the mare always stated that she resembled the Morgans of the time and was not typical of the Thoroughbred in appearance.

When mature Gifford was a very much admired horse, for he possessed to marked degree the lofty head carriage and stylish action that made the Morgans so popular. He was a fine saddle horse who loved the parades and musters which gave him the opportunity to show off his fine action and appearance. Like his sire he was completely fearless in the vicinity of cannons or muskets; the din of them merely caused him to prance and toss his finely chiseled head with

GIFFORD MORGAN JR (*Munson's*), *from Linsley*.

enthusiasm. However he was a gentle and completely trustworthy stallion at all times.

Gifford measured an even 14.2 in height and weighed about 1,000 pounds in his best condition. His head distinctly showed the Thoroughbred-Arab blood which his pedigree indicated: it was exceedingly fine, with large lively eyes and flaring nostrils and a dished profile so typical of the Arab. His neck was short and heavily crested with a lovely arched line from poll to wither. He had a deeper chest than his sire and his quarters were heavily muscled and strong. His tail, in the style of the time, had been docked, leaving the bone only about seven inches long, but despite this, the hair was thick and wavy. He had the typical good bone and feet of the new breed and was never unsound or blemished even though, as with the other horses of his time, his life was far from easy. Gifford was not liberally marked with white, having only a small star and snip and white pasterns behind and a white coronet on his right forefoot.

At the age of four years Gifford was purchased by Ira Coolidge of Barnard, Vermont. He remained in Barnard for four years, and then was bought back by Gifford, his breeder. From then until he was sixteen years old he was ridden, driven and used at the stud by his owner. He returned to Barnard under the ownership of Russell Topliff, who kept him until the horse was twenty years old. Only $100 was the price paid for the old horse when he was sold again, at twenty, and was taken into the state of New York. In his many years in the stud, old Gifford left much good stock all around the vicinity of his various homes. He commanded a very small fee and it is said that many a fine colt or filly cost its owner little more than fifty cents or a bushel or two of corn.

After the old stallion was sold into New York, F. A. Weir of Walpole, New Hampshire, became interested in the get of the horse and went to some lengths trying to locate him. He finally found Gifford in a little town near Lake George, New York. The old horse had come into hard times and was being used to draw slabs for a sawmill. He was weary, very poor and footsore, so Weir was able to buy him for the hundred dollars he'd sold for in the previous fall. Upon getting the old horse home to Walpole, he treated the animal for the lameness he suffered, the cause of which was a bad case of corns.

Weir is said to have secreted Gifford into the town late at night so no one would see the old fellow in such poor shape. Evidently he kept the old horse under wraps until such time he was sound and feeling his old self again, for when Gifford had recovered from the corns and was back in condition, Weir had quite a lark parading the stallion through the streets of Walpole, astonishing the villagers with the horse's style and animation.

For the next four years Gifford was a very popular sire in the neighboring countryside. He was bred to more than twenty mares a year at a fee of $30 (some improvement over the previous bushel of corn!). All during the four years that Weir owned him Gifford was shown quite extensively despite his advanced age.

GEN. GIFFORD

106

WILL stand for the use of Mares, this sea-son, at the stable of the subscriber, in Williamstown, Vt. The said Horse is six years old, and was sired by the OLD GIFFORD, of Walpole, who was sired by the celebrated BURBANK, or as sometimes called, the WOODBURY HORSE. All lovers of Morgan horses would do well to call and examine for themselves. The dam of the GEN. GIFFORD was also sired by the BUR-BANK—which makes him as full a blooded Morgan Horse as now lives. She was taken from Woodstock, Vt., in the year 1837, to Malden, Mass., and purchased by a gentleman for $250, and in 1842 she was purchased by the subscriber of Lally Eaton, of So. Reading, Mass., and taken to Croydon, N. H. She then weighed 1000 pounds, and for beauty and speed, if equalled, was never ex-celled, by any Morgan Mare.

It has been said by some French Canadian horse men who have sailed under the Morgan flag, that he was not as full a blooded Morgan horse as could be found. The subscriber would say that he will pay those men, or any gentleman, ONE HUNDRED DOLLARS if the blood of said Horse is not substantially correct. Now, Gentlemen, had you not better call and examine said Horse for yourselves, before putting your Mares other wheres, and losing the use of them and $25 with it.

ARIAL HALL.

Williamstown, May 18, 1855.

At the New York State Fair of 1847 in Saratoga old Gifford, along with a cavalcade of other Morgans, was paraded by the grandstand for all to see. It is reported that he had even then all the sprightly action and gaiety of a horse of six instead of an old granddad of twenty-three. Behind him in the cavalacade was his most famous son, HALE's GREEN MOUNTAIN MORGAN, as well as other fine sons and daughters.

Despite his spirit and animation old Gifford was extremely gentle and easily handled. Weir took much pleasure in walking into a show ring with the old stallion moving along beside him without a strap or bit of any kind on him. Then he would put the horse through his paces by oral commands alone, while Gifford moved about the ring as full of fire and vigor as a colt. And after the show when Weir loaded his equipment, old Gifford would follow in the same way in the manner of a big friendly dog. Needless to say, the old horse had many fond admirers and was an exceedingly popular horse.

As well as being popular, Gifford was also very prolific: his progeny have been estimated to number 1,300!

When he was twenty-four old Gifford was sold by Weir to a stock company in Walpole for the considerable sum of $2,000. However he got very few colts after he was sold and two years later, at the age of twenty-six, he died. His passing was a great loss to the Morgan breed.

HALE'S GREEN MOUNTAIN MORGAN

Perhaps the best known of the old-type Morgans was Hale's Green Mountain Morgan. A show horse in every sense of the word and a model for the so-called true type, his likeness appears on the top of today's Morgan registration certificate as the personification of the ideal. In the show rings of his time Green Mountain Morgan was known from Vermont to Kentucky to Michigan, for he was probably shown more extensively than any Morgan of his day. In the above-mentioned states, as well as in Ohio, he won championships at the state fairs, and his beauty and breeding were highly praised. Like his sire, he, too, created much interest when used for the frequent musters and military reviews in his home state.

HALE'S GREEN MOUNTAIN MORGAN

Stockmen all over New England who knew the Green Mountain Morgan had nothing but the highest praise for the horse. He was said by many to be the best stock horse, i.e., breeding stallion, in all New England at that time, and his sons were in much demand with substantial price tags on them all.

Silas Hale, under whose ownership the horse gained his greatest fame, says in a circular about the Green Mountain Morgan printed in 1853:

"The proprietor several years since becoming familiar with the peculiar experience of the Morgan race of horses, their speed, bottom, fitness for general practical service, their high spirit combined with docility and tractableness . . . which makes [them] perfectly reliable in all situations, was induced to inquire for a high-blood Morgan stallion, for the purpose of sending mares to him and improving the breed of horses in his vicinity. The horse formerly known by the name, 'Young Woodbury' and owned by John Woodbury of Bethel, Vermont, attracted his attention and he sent several mares to him, the colts from which gave early indications of valuable qualities. Afterwards the proprietor carefully examined the Young Woodbury and many of his colts in the vicinity of Bethel, which examination impressed him so favorably as to induce him to purchase the horse at a high price, which horse is now known by the name, 'Green Mountain Morgan.' Since said horse has been in the possession of the proprietor, he has had a liberal patronage and himself and his stock are become widely known and are highly valued. Several stallions begotten by the Green Mountain Morgan have been sold as high as fifteen hundred dollars each; many stallions of his get have brought prices ranging from eight to twelve hundred dollars each; numbers of geldings and mares of his get have been sold from three hundred to eight hundred dollars each; and many of them have proved very fast and but few of his colts, when matured, have been sold for less than two hundred dollars each.

"With regard to the pedigree of the Green Mountain Morgan, the proprietor has to say that he has conversed with quite a number of elderly persons who were acquainted with the original or Justin Morgan horse, with the stock immediately descended from him and with the sire and dam of the Green Mountain Morgan and who say that the Green Mountain Morgan strikingly illustrates the peculiar qualities of the original stock."

Green Mountain Morgan was foaled around 1832. The exact date of his birth is not known. He was born the property of George Bundy of Bethel, Vermont, but was bred by Nathaniel Whitcomb of Stockbridge. He was seal-brown in color, and when mature was 14.2 hands high and probably weighed about 1,100 pounds. His dam was a dark bay and said to have been by Woodbury; but nothing definite is really known about her except that she was purchased at Nashua, New Hampshire, by Whitcomb. At the time Whitcomb took a fancy to her she was working on the canal there. She was a low, thick-set mare, exceedingly strong and well muscled but not possessing much in the way of good looks. She was a bit long in the tooth when bred to old Gifford. After foaling Green Mountain Morgan she was sold and nothing more is known of her.

Green Mountain Morgan was only four months old when he was weaned and sold to David Gray of Stockbridge for $25. Gray kept the horse until the stallion was a four-year-old, when he made $50 on him by selling him to Hiram Twitchell of Bethel for $75. The horse became the property of John Woodbury shortly afterward.

Someone had been remiss about the horse's training along the way, for Woodbury, on trying to drive the stallion, found him ugly and contrary. He made several attempts to straighten the horse out but to no avail. The following spring, however, Woodbury decided to have another go at educating his purchase. Again he tried to drive the stallion (what preparations were made we have no way of knowing). This time he hitched him to a harrow and began to work him in a field bordering a river. But the horse got away from him and plunged into the river, to be held fast by the harrow to which he was still attached. The cold water foundered him badly and he was very lame for several months. Meanwhile Woodbury leased the stallion for stud purposes in Springfield, Vermont, where gradually he returned to a sound condition.

It was in 1842 when Silas Hale paid the $700 for him and brought the horse, now ten years old, home to South Royalston, Massachusetts. He kept the horse for eight years. The stallion must have improved much in appearance and way of going for it was during this time that he was shown so extensively.

Hale took Green Mountain Morgan west in 1853 and showed him at the state fairs of Kentucky, Ohio and Michigan where, as mentioned above, the horse won first premiums and much acclaim by all who saw him. In 1854 he won the first premium at the Vermont State Fair in Brattleboro. Only rarely was he ever beaten in compe-

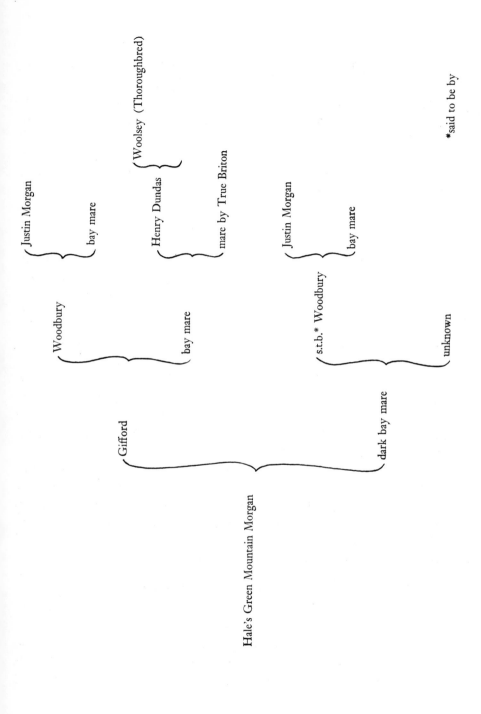

Hale's Green Mountain Morgan

Gifford
{
  Woodbury
  {
    Justin Morgan
    bay mare
  }
  bay mare
  {
    Henry Dundas
    {
      Woolsey (Thoroughbred)
      mare by True Briton
    }
  }
}
dark bay mare
{
  s.t.b.* Woodbury
  {
    Justin Morgan
    bay mare
  }
  unknown
}

*said to be by

tition; on one occasion by the famous Black Hawk at Rutland, Vermont.

When he was twenty-eight years old Green Mountain made one of his last appearances in the show ring in Woodstock, Vermont, in 1860. Heading a group of his best sons, the old stallion put on a great show for the spectators. He tossed his head like a colt and pranced about the ring, showing off all his fine qualities despite his advanced age. In his later years his disposition had mellowed and was such as to leave little to be desired. His manners also had improved to a point where he could stand or go through his paces on command without benefit of halter or bridle.

The best advertisement for the get of Green Mountain Morgan was the horse himself. Silas Hale evidently knew this full well, for everywhere the horse was shown, horsemen were putting in their orders for Green Mountain colts. Needless to say, the demand far exceeded the supply. Prices for the colts of this popular horse were far above the average of the day. A $1,500 horse would have the towns-folk goggle-eyed!

When you consider that the stud fee on Green Mountain Morgan was a mere $20 and that very few mature horses by him sold under $200 minimum (this being almost three times the general average sale price for the time), it is easy to realize the horse's great popularity as a stud.

Green Mountain Morgan's colts sold especially well on the farms and were considered the Vermonters' ideal. For the city markets they may have been regarded a bit small in size, but with their good legs and feet and natural agility they were much in demand for local work. Of course not to be underestimated was their bright good looks, which enhanced their value as well, for it was certainly no disgrace to drive to church behind a snappy Morgan even though all the week the same horse had been skidding logs or pulling a plow.

As far as beauty went, the Green Mountain colts had it aplenty. Their short, dished faces and big expressive eyes, their crested and smoothly arched necks and their close-ribbed, short, round bodies lent a symmetry which could not be overlooked. No wonder all who had seen the old Green Mountain were clamoring for his colts. And even with the beauty went the strong legs which were equal to any task: for they were known to be "all-day" driving horses who would come in at night with a spring in their step and light in their eyes. Small they were in stature, but with hearts as big as the new country they were helping to develop.

Years after his death Green Mountain was still considered the finest of the early Morgans. He lived to be thirty years old and left behind him some of the best examples of the Morgan breed to carry on for him in establishing a great line.

V

Descendants of Bulrush:

The Morrills

E VEN from its earliest beginnings in the rugged, windswept hills
of New Hampshire and Vermont, the Morgan horse was never
without its ardent admirers. The northcountry men of the soil, wise
in the ways of the conditions in which they lived, knew instinctively
that the qualities in evidence in the first Morgans were made-to-
order for their way of life. As the Morgans increased in numbers
through the efforts of these men, they found great favor with the folk
of the surrounding countryside.

At this time Morgans were virtually confined in their usefulness
to the farm and the road. Endurance and strength mattered more
than speed, and hardiness more than beauty, and these leading virtues the Morgans had in abundance. That the early horses of the
breed also possessed beauty and a certain ability to burn up the road
when necessary was another mark chalked up in their favor, for
who could resist a bit of a contest on the highway when the occasion
demanded? There was little enough recreation in a difficult life of
trying to scrape a living from a rocky side-hill farm.

Farmers raised Morgans because the hardy little animals were
their type of horse. They respected the Morgans' abilities, and
cleared their land and plowed their tilting fields and yet never tried
to conceal their pride in the fact that here were horses which could
not only work so willingly and successfully but could, when hitched
to the Sunday rig, hold up their heads and trot down the road with

snap in their gait and a full measure of proud beauty in their every line. And knowing that a turn of speed was available when needed made many a farmer sit straighter in his seat when passing a neighbor on the road.

But speed, while appreciated, was nonetheless not paramount with the men of the northcountry. Farmers had little time for developing race horses; and as far as the roads were concerned, one has only to scan a topographical map of the area to see that the roads, such as they were, were hardly conducive to the racing of horses to any great extent. And as for race tracks, at that time Vermont had none worthy of the name. So the Morgan was bred for and became the all-purpose horse of New England. His great endurance became his greatest asset and he toiled with his equally rugged human companions in the development of a new and difficult land.

THE NEW DEPARTURE

This, then, was the condition of the Morgan horse during its beginnings as a breed, prior to the 1840s. Then gradually, with the improvement of roads and the demand for harness horses which could move at a faster clip, it became evident to breeders that in order to sell their horses profitably the animals would have to be able to show ever-increasing speed at the trot. The lanky Messengers were appearing on the scene to challenge the Morgans' position on the road, a position which had seemed so firmly established. The Messengers, offspring of an imported English horse of primarily Arabian (Thoroughbred) breeding, were becoming increasingly popular.

Now the trouble began.

Where, before, breeders of Morgans made attempts to keep returning to the blood of the original Justin Morgan by selecting mares of that blood wherever possible, the new demand for speed and its attendant cry for greater size caused outside blood to find its way into the breed. Although recognizing the fact that endurance was still the greatest selling point in the Morgans' favor, nevertheless farmers and other breeders were tempted to outcross to other blood in an attempt to satisfy the desire for horses which were larger and faster. That many of the fine characteristics of the Morgan were lost in this experiment was a source of great consternation to many breeders who considered tampering with the breed a grave mistake. Luckily, back in the hills there were enough farmers who, unaffected by the popular demand, continued to breed Morgans as Morgans and considered the original characteristics of the breed far more important than the craze for speed.

By this time—the late '40s and '50s—the fame of the Morgan had spread all over the young and growing nation and animals of the breed were in great demand to assist in opening up and developing the sprawling new land. As comparatively few Morgans were to be had, due to the fact that they were being raised only in moderate numbers and for the most part in the back country of Vermont and New Hampshire, the demand greatly exceeded the supply. The result was, of course, an increasingly high price tag on good individuals such as has been noted concerning the get of Green Mountain Morgan.

Linsley, quoting from *The Maine Farmer* around 1850, says, pertaining to price and demand for Morgans: "For a seller of horses, it is only necessary for him to establish the fact that his horses are of the Morgan blood and he meets with a ready sale at good prices and the purchasers are more than satisfied."

Another result of the increasing country-wide demand for Morgans was the selling of outstanding stallions and mares for breeding

Young Morrill (Perkins')

Old Morrill

Jennison Horse

Randolph Morgan

Bulrush by Justin Morgan

dam untraced

black or brown mare, s.t.b.* Canadian stock

gray mare

Farrington Horse

Vance Horse by Bold Phoenix

unknown

bay mare

Kittredge Horse by Quicksilver by Imported Arabian

unknown

brown mare

Josiah Hoyt Horse

Bailey Horse

Woodbury by Justin Morgan

Dutch mare

unknown

gray mare, pedigree unknown

*said to be

stock to be shipped outside New England. The tour of Hale's Green Mountain through Ohio, Kentucky and Michigan was one example of how the excellence of the Morgan horse was successfully advertized to people who previously had little knowledge of the breed.

Buyers from the south and the west began trekking to Vermont to offer farmers and breeders very high prices for their best animals. Tempted by the jingle of silver many a breeder parted with some of his best stock, an action which soon resulted in lessening the quality of his herd. It is an obvious fact that unless some of the best individuals raised by a stock farm are retained for use by that farm, superior animals can hardly be expected to appear in its future breeding program.

This fact soon became apparent to many wide-awake breeders of Morgans during this period and, by turning down all offers on their best animals, they began producing first-rate Morgans in large enough numbers to be able to spare some for market.

THE MORRILL FAMILY

The Morgans of this period were used for the most part as road and business horses as well as for farm work. Some were occasionally raced. Their natural speed, which was a definite characteristic of the breed, was developed as had not been done in the early days and Morgans, more and more, became noted for this speed as well as for their endurance, spirit and beauty. The outcrossing of Morgans with the Messenger and later Hambletonian line also brought about a certain type of road horse that was different from the old-type Morgans and yet was still known as Morgan. These were used and trained as horses for the trotting tracks, and while some great individuals were produced they differed greatly from the original Vermont Morgans and were Morgans, really, in name only.

One family of Morgans which succumbed almost entirely to the influence of outside blood were the MORRILLS. Tracing in lineage to Bulrush, they possessed as a family the inherent substance and stamina which was so evident in Bulrush himself. They were bred from good road and work mares and were not high-strung and nervous as some lines tended to be. It is unfortunate, but all the good qualities

WINTHROP MORRILL *by Perkins' Young Morrill.*

of the Morrills are almost completely lost to the Morgan breed: after an all-too-brief day in the limelight they were bred to the lanky Hambletonians and, losing their identity, were absorbed by the new Standardbred breed. That they strengthened the Standardbred there is no room for argument, but they did so to their own eventual abdication as Morgans.

Randolph Morgan

The beginning of the Morrill line was Bulrush's best son, the stallion RANDOLPH MORGAN. He had a string of aliases to rival any Post Office "wanted" poster, for he was also called, Morgan Bulrush, Little Bulrush, the Weston horse, the Edson horse, etc., etc. He was very much like his sire, being a brown bay with a small star, and standing about 14.2. His mane and tail were thick and bushy, although in appearance he was possibly more finished and less drafty than Bulrush. But in endurance the Randolph Morgan could rival his sire, for no task, however tough, could wear him out. He was said to have drawn two men in a two-wheeled chaise eighty miles in one day without a sign of fatigue! A three-minute mile was considered lightning speed in the 1830s but the Randolph Morgan, boasting a great trot, could keep well within that time. All who knew him agreed that he was a very handsome horse of Morgan type and a great trotter for his day.

Little is known about the dam of the Randolph Morgan. She might have been a daughter of old Justin, as she originated from the vicinity of Randolph, Vermont, where the old horse had left many foals. At any rate, her son, foaled about 1820, was the image of Justin—possibly even more so than Bulrush himself.

The Jennison Colt

When the Randolph Morgan was bred, in 1840, to a large Canadian-bred mare (of unknown ancestry but possessing a certain ability at drawing timber from the Randolph woods), the result was a cherry-bay foal called the JENNISON COLT. At maturity this colt, the spit and image of his sire but the size and weight of his dam, was considered a fine horse and the proverbial pride and joy of his owner, Abijah Jennison. To quote Jennison, speaking of his colt:

"When he was foaled, well, the best description of him I can give is that he was perfect and he grew perfect. He weighed over 1,200 pounds and was a bright bay, no white on him but a little star, and he had the same little, short, sharp, quick ear of the little Morgan [presumably Randolph Morgan]. His mother had pretty long ears and they lapped some [an interesting note]; and he had a wide forehead and his eyes were large and stood out and he had just such a foretop, mane, and tail as the little Morgan. Oh, he was the little Randolph all over except his size; and he took that from his mother. I had the colt when he was two years old and that was the season he sired Old Morrill."

VERMONT MORRILL.

PEDIGREE

VERMONT MORRILL was sired by the trotting stallion, so widely known and justly celebrated throughout the New England States, called the *Morrill Horse*, raised and now owned by FRENCH MORRILL, at Danville, Vt.,—he by the *Jennison Horse*,—he by the *Old Morgan Bulrush*,—and he by the original *Justin Morgan*. The dam of *Morrill Horse* is one of the finest specimens of breeding mares in Vermont, and a true descendant of the Imported *Messenger*.

VERMONT MORRILL is 5 years old this spring---is of a jet black color---15½ hands high---weighs 1050 lbs., and has already trotted A MILE IN THREE MINUTES, without training.

The Dam of **VERMONT MORRILL** is an excellent breeding mare, owned by Mr. Nathan Way, of Peacham, Vt., and is derived from the Sherman Morgan Stock,—by which it is seen that this horse combines the blood of two of the best branches of the Morgan race, with a genuine mixture of the Messenger.

CERTIFICATE

The undersigned, citizens of Danville, Caledonia Co. Vermont, hereby certify, that we know the horse above described, owned by Mr. John S. Way, and positively know him to be a Colt of the original MORRILL HORSE.

FRENCH MORRILL, Owner of Morrill Horse.
G. A. BURBANK, County Clerk.
J. S. H. WEEKS, Merchant.
VAIL BRAINERD & CO., Merchants.

SAM'L B. MATTOCKS, Cashier.
H. C. BABCOCK, Merchant.
SARGENT FIELD, Ex. Sheriff Cal. Co.
GEO. D. LADD, Attorney at Law.

WM. B. PALMER, Merchant.
JAMES GUILD, Merchant.
ANDREW M. WEST, Tinsmith.
ROYAL M. AYER, Physician.
AARON H. SMITH, Farmer.

☞ All lovers of good Horses are invited to examine young VERMONT MORRILL, as the owner confidently believes that a personal inspection by good judges will prove a better recommend than anything that can be written.

VERMONT MORRILL will stand for the use of Mares this Season as follows :---

Mondays,
Tuesdays,
Wednesdays,

Thursdays,
Fridays,
Saturdays,

TERMS---

St. Anthony's Falls, Minnesota Territory, May 1, 1855.

JOHN S. WAY.

Printed by BALLOU & LOVELAND, Montpelier, Vt.

Outcrossing to Messenger blood is a selling point in this 1855 poster.

It is easy to see from the statement above that Abijah Jennison was very fond of the big bay colt. This fact must have made it quite difficult for him when, being a poor man, he was forced to sell his young stud as a three-year-old. Somehow he managed to buy him back two years later, only to have to part with him again due to a pathetic lack of funds. This is the last that is ever heard of the Jennison horse, although some say he was sold to a New Hampshire stock farm. At any rate, nothing is definite.

Old Morrill

OLD MORRILL, by the Jennison horse—whose stud fee it is reported was a pound of tea!—was foaled late in 1843. He was seal-brown in color, although some describe him as black with tan muzzle and flanks. He had a white right hind sock and at maturity stood 15.3 and weighed about 1,225 pounds. His dam was gray. She was a very well-bred mare, being seven-eighths Thorougbhred; she stood 15.2, had a long neck, moderately lengthy head and ears and a fine coat through which the veins showed prominently. She was purchased by James Heath of Walden, Vermont, as a two-year-old. Despite the fact that shortly afterward she fractured one of her hind legs, which, though it healed, left her with a distinct hitch in her gait, she was very good in harness and was known to have cleared Heath's rough, side-hill farm. Some work for a crippled mare of Thoroughbred blood!

Morrill was a composite of the breeding behind him. He was fine-coated, and unlike his Morgan forebears had a scant mane and tail. His head was excellent, with fine ears and large eyes, although something of his granddam showed up in his hairy jaw and shaggy fetlocks. His feet were large and his pasterns a bit short, but he was a strong, energetic horse with a pure trotting gait that was as speedy as it was balanced. He was a rare combination of speed and strength and was considered at the time to have no equal in New England in this respect.

Morrill was sold as a weanling to Urban Perkins of South Walden, Vermont, and was later traded to French Morrill, in neighboring Danville, when four years old. Until he was seven Morrill was

used as a buggy horse and worked in a team on the farm. He was used regularly at stud as well, before being sold for the rumored price of $1,000 to a man in Massachusetts. However back he came to Vermont shortly afterward, when the Massachusetts man proved unable to pay for him. There he remained under the ownersership of Morrill until he died at the age of nineteen in 1862.

Young Morrill, Winthrop and Fearnaught

Most of Old Morrill's Vermont sons and daughters lived out their lives on the farms of the region in the traditional Morgan manner: as driving horses and for farm work. But the old horse sired also a prolific line of race horses which subsequently were the ones to become absorbed into the Standardbred breed.

Old Morrill sired the bay PERKINS' YOUNG MORRILL, his best son, who was foaled in 1850. Young Morrill in turn sired FEARNAUGHT and WINTHROP MORRILL, two of the very best trotters of the century. Winthrop Morrill, even though bred to ordinary farm mares, stood fifth on the list of sires of 2:30 performers (horses which could trot the mile in two minutes, thirty seconds). Fearnaught at one time brought the fabulous sum of $25,000 and was Grand Champion Trotting Stallion of the World in 1868. He was a very successful sire and commanded a fee of $250, a substantial amount for any stud in those days.

Young Morrill also sired DRACO (2:28½) and DANVILLE BOY, two racing champions of the day.

As a family the Morrills were larger in all respects than the early Morgans. Their absorption into the Standardbred *Register* took place when breeders, finding the speedy, line-bred Messengers lacking in racing stamina, crossed them with the Morrills to make up the deficit. Gradually the Morgan blood, thinned by an ever-increasing amount of the Messenger-Hambletonian, was lost till it became unrecognizable. But the blood was there, though diluted, and the establishment of the Standardbred horse owes much to the Morgans of the Morrill line.

VI

Type, Conformation and Action

FROM the descriptions of the most prominent and outstanding Morgan stallions during the formative years of the breed, it is easily noted that their type and conformation was remarkably uniform, except, possibly, in regard to height. Here there was a marked variation in some families; for example, it is noticed that the Morrills tended to be larger and more rangy than the Woodburys. However the early Morgans possessed many characteristics in common—enough, certainly, to establish them as a type and an up-and-coming new breed: fine heads with small ears, prominent eyes and large nostrils, symmetrical bodies, cresty necks and good legs and feet were typical of the Morgan then as now.

Certainly the fact that there was no breed *Register* before 1894—and that, as shown earlier, outcrossing to other than Morgan blood was frequent and neither condoned nor condemned in most cases—makes the continuance of the Morgan breed seem even more remarkable. Without rules to govern the breeding of Morgan horses as a definite type, it is certainly surprising that the breed did not disappear altogether before the Morgan *Register* and the Morgan Club were established. The use of Standardbred stallions and mares indeed almost did spell *finis* to the Morgan during the latter part of the 1800s. As happened with the Morgans' loss of the Morrill family to the Standardbred, so could the remnants of the breed have been ab-

IDEAL MORGAN MARE

sorbed into another and lost for all time. But for a few breeders who were dedicated to the Morgan as a separate entity and bred him as such—and not merely for his fine qualities which might mix well with another breed—the Morgan might today be as extinct as the quagga.

That the breed type has been preserved and even strengthened can be seen by the splendid examples of the Morgan in evidence at horse shows and breeding farms the country over. And Morgan type is perhaps more clearly defined and understood today than it was in the earlier days of the breed.

IDEAL MORGAN STALLION

Yet in recent years Morgan type has been an explosive subject whenever breeders congregate, for each has his own opinion as to the ideal and his own ideas on the best bloodlines to use to obtain this ideal. Because different bloodlines have produced variations in type and each breeder feels he is producing the *only* true type, often a discussion of Morgan type will generate a considerable amount of heat.

But as before, the Morgan horse has always managed to survive the perils of human errors, and today with a *Register* and a breed association to "make the rules," Morgans are in better condition as a breed than they have ever been in their history.

TYPE

No one really knows just exactly what old Justin Morgan looked like; we can only guess at his actual appearance. Yet today, except for size, we have stallions of the breed which fit his description to the letter. A clearer and clearer picture of the ideal in Morgan type is emerging from the battles and the conflicts and only the die-hards refuse to recognize it.

In every breed of livestock—whether it be Suffolk sheep or Hereford cattle or Dalmatian dogs—this ideal type or breed standard is considered on equal footing with the health and constitution of the animal. It is the point breeders and stockmen will look for first: whether or not the animal conforms to its breed standard of perfection as closely as possible. Conformation, or bone structure, are of course of prime importance; but an animal can be a finely conformed one and still not meet the standard of perfection of its breed.

Standard of Perfection of the Morgan Horse

So it is with Morgan horses. Yet it was not until recent years that there was enough agreement among breeders for The Morgan Horse Club to set up the Standard of Perfection that is given now:

HEIGHT: 14.1 to 15.1 with 14.3 considered the ideal by many.

WEIGHT: 900 to 1,100 pounds.

GENERAL CONFORMATION: Good saddle conformation. In general the Morgan should be compact, of medium length, well muscled, smooth and stylish in appearance.

QUALITY: The Morgan should have clean, dense bone with sufficient substance; well-developed joints and tendons, and a fine coat.

TEMPERAMENT: The Morgan should be tractable but with good spirit.

HEAD AND NECK: *Head*—Medium size, clean cut and tapering from the jaw to the muzzle. It should be wide between the eyes, long from ear to eye, short from eye to nostril. The profile can be straight or slightly dished but *never* Roman-nosed. The lower jaw should be wide and clean cut and the muzzle fine with small, firm lips and large nostrils. The eyes should be large, dark and prominent, set well out on the sides of the head. The ears should be small, fine-pointed, set wide apart and always carried alertly. *Neck*—Medium in length, well crested on top, straight on the bottom line; clean cut at the throatlatch. It should be smoothly joined to the shoulder and deep at the point of the shoulder. The crest should form a smooth curve from poll to withers. The mane and foretop should be full.

FOREHAND: *Shoulders*—Long, with good angulation. They should blend smoothly with the neck into well-defined but medium-high withers. The withers should be slightly higher than the point of the hip. *Forelegs*—Fairly short, squarely set, well apart, with short muscular arms. Viewed from the front, the legs should be thin and must be straight; viewed from the side should be wide and sinewy. *Forearm*—Wide, flat and muscular. Knees should be wide and flat. *Cannon*—Wide from the side, thin from the front and relatively short. *Fetlock joints*—Rather wide but not round. *Pasterns*—Clean and strong, of medium length, the slope to correlate with the slope of the shoulder. *Feet*—Medium size, nearly round, open at the heel, smooth and dense but not brittle.

BODY: The body conformation of the Morgan is distinctive, with *chest* of good depth and width; with the *back* short, broad and well muscled. The *loin* should be wide and muscular and closely coupled. The *barrel* should be large and rather round, with well-sprung, closely-joined ribs and deep full flank.

HINDQUARTERS: *Hind legs*—Squarely set and so placed that he turns on his hindquarters with legs well under him. *Hips*—Well rounded; hip bones should never show. *Croup*—Rounded gently with a fairly high-set tail, well carried. *Tail*—Long and full. *Quarters and thighs*—Deep and well muscled with strong stifles and medium-length, wide, muscular gaskins. *Hocks*—Wide, deep and clean; viewed from the rear, the hind legs should be perpendicular, with the hocks neither closer together nor wider apart than the fetlocks. *Cannons*—Short, wide and flat, with the tendons standing well out from the bone and well defined. *Pasterns*—Strong, medium length and not too sloping. *Hind feet*—Resembling the forefeet and round, medium in size, smooth and dense.

ACTION: The natural gaits of the Morgan horse are the walk, trot and canter. *Walk*—Flatfooted, elastic and rapid with a long, straight, free stride. *Trot* must be square, free-going, collected and balanced. *Canter* must be smooth, easy, collected and straight on both leads.

Time Out for Controversy

Basically every breeder of Morgan horses today has, in his own mind, a definite ideal or aim. His breeding program is not just hit or miss, but is the result of study and thoughtful planning. Each breeder knows the type of Morgan he is trying to raise, and the type of potential buyer he wishes to attract.

If he is in the Western states, it is reasonable to expect that he is producing a Morgan which in both conformation and temperament will be suitable for use as a working stock horse and/or for Western trail and pleasure riding. He will be producing Morgans which are rugged and even-tempered and hardy. He will not be as interested in his Morgans' having high action or the utmost in quality; indeed he may even *prefer* a horse that has heavier bone and a tendency to grow a thick, long coat in the winter. He may expect his horses to lead a rugged life, out of doors most of the time and working long hours carrying a rider over rough country. Certainly he would not expect this same horse to perform in a fancy show ring with all the fire and brilliance of the Morgans bred for this purpose. Therefore in his breeding program he is striving for Morgans which are mentally and physically qualified for the life they are to lead.

Now, the Eastern breeder may not be interested in a heavy, stock-horse type of Morgan. His aims may be different. He may wish to produce Morgans of the show-ring type where refinement and sprightly action are required.

Yet the versatility within the Morgan breed makes it possible for each breeder to raise Morgans which are his pleasure and yet still have them conform *basically* to the general type. That some blood-lines produce one type and others a different one has always been apparent. The catch would seem to be that at times even the most careful mating can produce a dud both in the case of the man striving to breed Morgan stock horses and of the fellow with Morgan show horses in mind. If these breeders had the courage to sell as grades the so-called duds or culls that weren't up to the standard, many problems within the breed would be avoided. The registering of horses which are far below the standard—either through lack of type or faulty conformation—just because they were purebred is a grave mistake, but one which just about every breeder makes. It is these registered culls that give a breed a bad name in many, many cases.

That each breeder is convinced that he is breeding the true-type Morgan is well-established fact. Yet the variations found in the breed tend to underline the fact that someone must be on the wrong track. The catch is, however, who is to say who is raising the wrong type of Morgan? Who is going to set himself up as the authority? There are many who are more than willing to do so; who can spout pedigrees and bloodlines with expert proficiency; who can condemn or praise a certain line of Morgans vehemently and lay down before you all the mistakes and blunders all other breeders have made since Woodbury was a colt! But are the Morgans these experts are producing necessarily the *best* Morgans available? Or are other less "expert" breeders, who quietly go their way studying the breed and producing consistently good colts without fanfare, also authorities?

So it would be only deluding ourselves to say that there is no dissention within the ranks on the subject of Morgan type. But we console ourselves with the fact that in every breed of horses, differences of opinion prevail among its breeders. The serious and damaging result of this wrangling among breeders is the effect it tends to have upon new people becoming interested in Morgans; and it does irreparable harm to the very breed it is trying to promote. It stands to reason that if John Smith wanted to buy himself and his family a registered horse, he would be mighty hesitant about purchasing an individual of a breed that has no standard which is completely acceptable to all. He will say, "Even they don't know what they are trying to establish, so how am I, a newcomer, to know?" This has been detrimental to many types of livestock and the battling and squabbling among breeders has led only to public confusion.

The Morgan horse, and on this *all* breeders agree, is the very best all-round breed for the general horse enthusiast. His versatility has

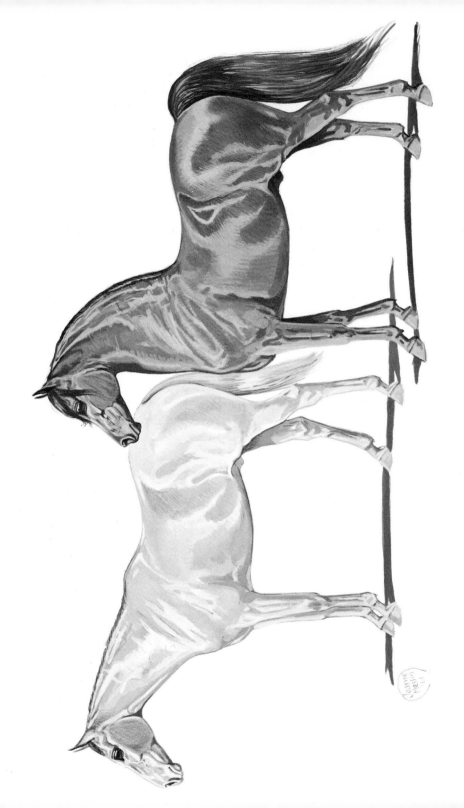

" . . . the Morgan Horse is one thing—every other kind of horse is something else."

been proved in innumerable ways, and as a pleasure horse he has no equal. Despite difficulties along the way, the Morgan has come through it all, increasing the number of his devotees every year. In this chapter we will try to give the best possible picture of the Morgan in hopes that those to whom he is an unfamiliar breed will have a clear understanding of his type, conformation and performance.

Size—and More Pros and Cons

When Justin Morgan trod the earth in the early 1800s folks found him able to handle just about any task despite his diminutive size. Yet many even in that day voiced the opinion that he and his descendants were too small and that they would be even more valuable if, with their other qualities, they "came in a larger size."

Of course there was a decided variation in size in the early Morgans as can be noted by a short perusal of the Morgan *Register*. Still, the best-type Morgans of the time were those which were not too large. An increase in size brought about by the use of outside blood from the mid-1800s to the present century proved to be detrimental to the Morgan, as many breeders were to learn. But since they were probably not so concerned with Morgan type as with Morgan aptitude, they outcrossed to cold blood for farm teams and to Messenger blood for trotting speed. The practice may have been frowned upon or not, but it continued nevertheless. It is a wonder that the Morgan breed ever survived during the days of the establishment of the Standardbred, for the demand for size as well as for trotting speed nearly proved the undoing of the Morgan.

Here would be a good place to pause for a quick rundown of the rules for admission to the Morgan *Register*. In Volume I (1894) "any animal in either of the following classes" was eligible for registry: "RULE I—Any meritorious stallion or mare that traces in direct male line to the original Justin Morgan Horse, and has at least *one sixty-fourth* of his blood" [italics mine]; and "RULE II—The produce of a sire and dam both registered in The Morgan Register."

However by 1905, when Volume II came out and breeders had had a decade to reconsider the leniency allowed in the matter of outside blood, the regulations were tightened somewhat: Rule I allowed registry to "any meritorious stallion, mare or gelding that traces in direct male line to Justin Morgan, and has at least one sixty-fourth of his blood: provided the dam and sire's dam were bred in approved speed or roadster lines."

Rule II granted eligibility to "any meritorious stallion, mare or gelding having *one thirty-second or more* [italics mine] of the blood of Justin Morgan: provided the sire and dam were bred in approved speed or roadster lines." Rule III repeated the second criterion laid down in 1894, i.e., that the produce of a sire and dam both carried in the *Register* was eligible.

The 1905 Rule II was rescinded as of January 1, 1948. Since then an X preceding a number in the *Register* indicates an inclusion prior to 1948 under this old rule, which allowed some animals to be registered although one parent was not itself registered in the AMHR. As can be seen readily, this rescinding really "closed the books," for subsequently only foals of registered Morgan sires and out of registered Morgan dams have been eligible for the AMHR.

In the darkest days of the breed—the early 1900s—with the appearance of the automobile and the subsequent disappearance of the harness road horse, the Morgan again was dealt a serious setback. Only the efforts of a few dedicated breeders and the U.S. Department of Agriculture's Morgan farm in Vermont saved the breed at all.

Included in the breeding program at the government farm were stallions which, along with their Morgan blood, traced to American Saddlebred and Thoroughbred blood. This blood was infused with the old Morgan blood to produce horses which were more saddle type and larger in many respects than the old Vermont Morgans. In the chapter describing the government farm, this breeding program is discussed in greater detail, so there is no need to go into it here. The point to be made, however, is that size was an important factor in the government's breeding program. Realizing that the Morgan had wonderful qualifications as a pleasure horse, efforts were being made there to produce Morgans which would be better animals for the trail or show ring, i.e., definite saddle rather than harness type.

It was during this time that the Morgan came into his new rôle as a pleasure horse. Size was important because of competition from other breeds. Older breeders of the Morgan objected heatedly to the government farm's use of Saddleblood, saying that the harm done outweighed the fact that Morgans were increasing in both popularity and numbers. The farm retaliated with the declaration that the Morgan was improved by the controlled quantity of outside blood. They felt that Morgan character was being retained in a modified form and that the twentieth-century markets were no longer dictating the raising of speedy road horses or harness-race horses—the automobile quelled the one and the Standardbred the other.

It was the differences of opinion over the outcrossing to Saddleblood that caused the first split in Morgan ranks, the proponents of the old type objecting to Saddleblood, the backers of the so-called new type accusing them, in turn, of being unrealistic.

This situation has come down to the present day with varying intensity. With the rescinding in 1948 of Rule II (which, as we have seen, allowed horses of unknown or other than Morgan blood to be included in the *Register*) it seemed that the situation would smooth itself out, as no further outside blood could be introduced into the breed. But many felt that irreparable damage had already been done.

As for the matter of size, it would seem that, all things considered, any Morgan which fit the description in the Standard of Perfection and was within the 14.1 to 15.1 height would not be too highly criticized, yet often there are great objections to Morgans which stand over 15 hands. The reason for this, possibly, is the fact that many individuals which are 15 hands or over, lack the other characteristics of the breed as well. From this the trouble stems, and the ideal in height was set within 14.1 to 15.1. The majority of breeders feel that 14.3 is the ideal height and many have a tendency to lean more toward the 15-hand mark rather than the 14. Many excellent-type individuals have been produced in recent years, however, which stand over 15 hands and still retain the best Morgan characteristics.

Old vs. New Type

First, on the touchy subject of type, it is best to say that most breeders of Morgans, despite some variation, are aiming for the best possible Morgans which are closest to the ideal in type as described in the Standard of Perfection. That this is being accomplished by conscientious breeders can be seen at the horse shows where Morgans are exhibited and on the stock farms, too.

With all outside blood now ruled out, Morgans bred *with thought and care* cannot help but return to the basic type of old Justin, with modern-day variations necessary for today's markets. Even in the last few years since Rule II was rescinded, Morgans are being raised that are superior in a great many ways to some of the early ones. They have quality and refinement as well as the character of the old type, and the best individuals show a successful blending of the old and the new.

The illustration given perhaps shows best the examples of (1) what is considered old type, (2) new type and (3) a blending of them both. Many breeders feel that the new Morgan is best suited to all of today's variety of uses, whether it be for stock work or the show ring. They maintain that, bred for substance and soundness as well as for the refinement which makes the Morgan of today so popular, it is only a matter of training to prove the Morgan's versatility. His type may vary slightly to suit his bent in life but basically the training he receives, not his type, will determine how versatile he will be. The illustrations and accompanying comments give more than words alone the variations in type in the Morgan horse.

CONFORMATION

Conformation, as any horseman knows, is even more basic than type in any breed. Good conformation is essential. If a horse—any horse of any breed—has a definite weakness in conformation, he should be overlooked as a breeding animal, regardless of whether he is "typy" or "showy." For to breed animals with glaring conformation faults is just ordering trouble no matter the pedigree. Never be sold on a stallion or mare that you wish to use for breeding before carefully going over its conformation, and even if the pedigree shows the highest percentage of Justin's blood beware if conformation faults are in evidence.

Old type (high percentage), circa 1880.

Modern Morgan of today.

So-called new type, circa 1930.

If a horse is structurally sound and shows no serious weakness he is a much better bet in a breeding program than one with type and a number of glaring weaknesses which he is likely to transmit. Too much stress on pedigree and surface beauty without careful consideration to conformation will undermine many a breeding program.

Percentage as a Factor

Most Morgans of today can be said to have just about 10 percent of the blood of Justin Morgan. A few may have 12 percent, but anything over 14 percent is very rare indeed. Yet there are breeders who insist that a high percentage of Justin Morgan blood is a virtual guarantee that the animal *must* be superior to one less endowed. High-percentage Morgans descend from only one early strain: that of Hale's Green Mountain, carried via ETHAN ALLEN 3RD, whose heyday was the 1890s and among whose ancestors—not including Justin, Sherman and Woodbury—were Gifford, Hale's Green Mountain, Peters' Vermont, Black Hawk, Ethan Allen I (50), Billy Root, Royal Morgan and Vermont Morgan Champion. With such a record it's perfectly safe to say that the best individuals come from this strain. However it is most important not to discount the other strains, because it is entirely possible—indeed it has been accomplished—to get fine individuals from less royally-bred lines.

It is a paradox, though, that occasionally the high-percentage Morgan can exhibit the certain coarseness in the head and throttle that is becoming more and more undesirable in modern Morgans. The animal is often comparatively small and, although possibly possessing type to a marked degree, is quite likely to lack the quality and refinement which is so sought-after nowadays. It is advisable to examine thoroughly any horse before purchasing him and there is no need to stress the point here. But keeping in mind that it takes more than high percentage and pedigree to make a fine horse, look at the horse *first* and the papers afterward! Pedigrees are important: certainly there is no argument there. But always bear in mind that it is a grave mistake to fall for the "percentage line" if the horse doesn't measure up to the true Morgan type promised by his papers.

Much has been discussed pertaining to the so-called X in modern Morgan pedigrees. The X beside a horse's name in a pedigree means that either one or both of its parents was of other than Morgan blood, i.e., either the blood of another registered breed or that of an unknown or a grade. As mentioned earlier in this chapter, many horses were admitted into the *American Morgan Horse Register* that were of outside blood when Rule II was introduced. After 1948, when it was rescinded, the horses bred with this outside blood were given Xs by their names to denote that they were products of this outcrossing.

An X can also be the result of a horse's being eligible for registration during this period but one whose owner failed to register.

Unless a few unscrupulous breeders, or those who fail to study the bloodlines of animals they employ for breeding, misuse the X in producing Morgans, it would seem that little harm can now be done by the X at this time. Of course any concentration of the blood of animals which carry Xs is going to result in a loss of type and Morgan characteristics. In other words, if a breeder has several mares in his herd which have Xs in their pedigrees, and he keeps breeding them to stallions with a fair amount of outside blood, then it has to follow that loss of type will be the result. This did happen to some extent in certain strains and much of that intangible something that is known as the "Morgan look" was lost.

Selection as a Factor

It is probably safe to say that the majority of breeders would prefer their Morgans to be of high-percentage blood, for they realize that true Morgan characteristics are produced through the concentration of this blood; but it is the wise breeder who selects carefully when mating animals of high-percentage pedigree because it is quite possible that even high-percentage horses have inherited a number of significant faults along with a generous measure of Morgan characteristics. As an example of this, say there is a fine high-percentage Morgan mare available for breeding. You like her looks in general but perhaps wish she had smaller ears and her bone was slightly flatter. She is basically a good Morgan, however, despite some coarseness about the head. Then you study her pedigree and find that there are several ancestors which have non-Morgan and unknown blood behind them.

Perhaps the coarser characteristics the mare displays have been transmitted to her through her grandparents or great-grandparents, a few of which were grades. Realizing that she is likely to transmit some of these undesirable characteristics to her offspring, you would wisely breed her to a stallion dominantly excellent in these points—regardless of whether he is high percentage himself. It would be only folly to breed your mare to another high-percentage stallion merely because he was high percentage, if that stallion lacks, in a similar way, the refinement you wish to see in the foal. And yet it is surprising how often this has been done in the breeding of modern Morgans by people to whom fancy bloodlines on paper are more enticing than actual excellence in an individual.

In all breeds of horses in all sections of the country, there are some breeders who put their main emphasis on pedigree. The breeder of Thoroughbreds for the race track breeds speed to speed, as it were; and if the results look like greyhounds instead of horses, what does it matter so long as they are fast? Type and breed characteristics matter little. For many years the Palomino was bred strictly for color, with conformation secondary; likewise the Appaloosa. Other stockmen concentrate on breeding their horses for a special use: for working stock horses, for example, and the pedigree is secondary.

The best practice with Morgans would seem to be a practical blending of importance placed on pedigree, type, conformation and the future use the resulting foal will be put to.

Returning for a moment to the subject of the X in a Morgan pedigree, there is one well-known case where a whole strain of fine Morgans was virtually built around an X pedigree. The X in this particular example designated the blood of registered American Saddlebreds tracing to Morgan lineage. It is interesting to note that not all individuals in this particular family were ideal in Morgan type, and many resembled Morgans not at all; yet with certain crosses to other Morgan blood the results were horses which became consistent winners in Morgan classes at the shows. Careful selection, using this Saddleblood judiciously, produced fine Morgan individuals which were winners in the ring under Morgan judges. A few members of this family lacked Morgan characteristics to a marked degree, while others were considered true in type. But in general the strain was and is noted for the quality and refinement it displays. A crossing of this blood with old Morgan blood seemed to have produced the best type for modern demands. A clear understanding of the reason for, and the meaning of, an X in a Morgan pedigree should result in Morgans of the modern type who will be good breeding prospects for the future despite their outside blood.

On the other hand, when dealing with Xs which designate unknown or grade blood (of no established breed), the controlling of its influence will be more difficult and often unsuccessful, because the breeder has no knowledge as to what traits might be recessive and could crop up in his colts from unknown ancestry. It is far easier to plan a breeding program when dealing with known factors than it is by using guesswork where the inheritance is doubtful. However here again there are groups within the Morgan ranks who actually prefer to have any Xs which might be found in a Morgan pedigree designate a grade or unknown rather than have the so-called taint of Saddleblood there. This group has a dedicated following among a few Morgan breeders, but the Morgans they produce are not necessarily any better than the ones produced by breeders who have wisely used the outcrossing to other recognized blood.

So to sum up: remember that high percentage is no *guarantee* of the excellence of an individual Morgan; that outside blood of a known breed (allowed by Rule II) has not "ruined" the breed and will not if handled wisely, and that the best rule to follow is to be selective and keep to the middle of the road and not veer off on a tangent either way!

ACTION

The action of the Morgan horse is as distinctive as his fine head and symmetrical appearance. The Morgan's short, nervous step with its impression of unlimited, pent-up energy is as typically Morgan as his cresty neck and his tiny ears. Some of the best examples of the breed possess this snappy way of going, but, as in body conformation, there are some variations in different individuals. The smaller Morgan is naturally going to have a shorter stride than the Morgan which stands 15 hands or better. The smaller horse possibly will give the impression of having a truer Morgan gait, in that it is likely to be more rapid and "trappy" as compared to that of the larger horse which has a naturally longer stride due to its greater length of leg. The small, chunky, short-legged Morgan of the old type, many say, has the so-called true Morgan way of going, and the larger horse moves more like a Saddlebred or Standardbred with a longer stride and less choppiness. This may be true: but it is a matter of preference to the breeder which type of action will suit his needs; and he raises his Morgans accordingly. Some say the short-strided, trappy way of going is the more typical of the Morgan horse—but it is not necessarily found in every Morgan; again it depends greatly on breeding. Nevertheless there is a definite spring in the step of every Morgan which sets him apart from other breeds. Given here are the three gaits as ideally performed by the Morgan horse.

THE WALK: In all cases the walk should be rapid and elastic, and it should give the impression of power and energy. The Morgan should carry his head up and his ears alert. Every movement should reveal his energetic enthusiasm. Never should a Morgan possess a plodding walk such as is often found in other breeds of light horses. He should naturally carry his head high and appear interested in the surroundings; this attitude is typical of the Morgan.

It is said by many that a Morgan truly shares experiences with his rider. He doesn't miss a trick, as the saying goes, and it certainly can be applied to Morgans, for they seem always to be interested and looking. Indeed, this sharing experiences and liking it, makes the Morgan the outstanding trail and pleasure horse he is. The companionship enjoyed with such a horse cannot be equaled, as many a Morgan owner will attest with enthusiasm.

THE TROT: The action of the Morgan at the trot should, in general, be smooth, collected and square, as stated in the Standard of Perfection. But of necessity there are definite variations according to conformation and use. The pleasure and trail horse must have a ground-covering, easy trot with a stride that is comfortable to his rider. Therefore less action is desired in a Morgan used primarily for pleasure and utility. This same horse, however, when collected

WALK

and brought up in the bridle, should possess a certain amount of natural inherent knee action. Morgans should have a snap to their knees and should not move, for instance, like a Thoroughbred which, with its "daisy clipping" action, barely skims the ground, not bending its knees any more than necessary.

That many Morgans possess remarkable ability for the high, showy action so sought after by show-ring enthusiasts is a definite asset to the breed. Since this action is often a matter of breeding, certain strains are much in demand by folks with a yen for the tanbark. It is a well-established fact that some lines—Woodbury, Gifford, Hale's Green Mountain—passed on this showy ability with remarkable consistency. And often little or no special training or shoeing is needed to bring it out. These are the Morgans that make a name for the breed in the show ring, for this sparkling action at the trot has great appeal. The illustrations show the trot, both in the pleasure Morgan and the show Morgan, indicating the difference in the use of the knees and shoulders at this gait.

Some breeders criticize the high action in Morgans and feel that it is only an imitation of the Saddlebred. But as was mentioned before, the natural high action is a definite characteristic of some bloodlines and cannot be taken away from them any more than it can be successfully put on them if they possess no natural aptitude. There is the case of one particular Morgan stallion of the purest Morgan bloodlines that stands but 14.2 and yet has the most beautiful naturally showy trot I have ever seen. He has never been trained for action and has been used on the trail and at various tasks with many different riders, yet in hand or under saddle he collects himself, and the brilliance of his trot is a joy to see. And he is all of sixteen years of age! This action is bred into him. His sire was noted for it as was his grandsire and his great-grandsire, and it could no more be taken away from him than could a part of his body.

All this boils down to the fact that the trot of the Morgan should be distinctive. In the pleasure horse it should be easy and ground-covering. In the Morgan bred for the show ring it should be high, but naturally so, with no indication of effort or artificiality.

In recent years—with the Morgan becoming increasingly popular in the show ring, especially in the East and Midwest—there has been a definite within-the-breed controversy over whether or not the Morgan should, for show-ring purposes, be made to grow a longer toe and wear weighted shoes to increase his action at the trot. Many feel that the practices, while increasing Morgan action, tend to make him more an imitation of the American Saddlebred rather than distinctly Morgan. However I believe that the majority feel that within reason any encouraging of the Morgan's built-in beauty of motion will be of value in the show ring. Much of the criticism has come from Morgan owners who use their horses for pleasure and/or pleasure classes

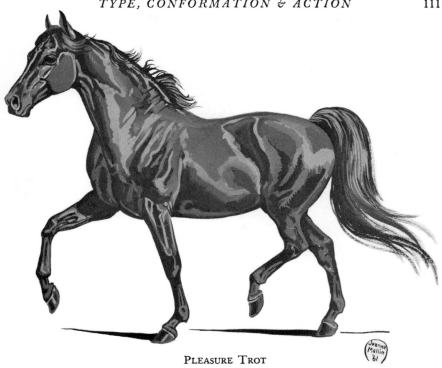

PLEASURE TROT

in the shows: they accuse the people who show Morgans in performance classes of ruining the breed by their use of heavier shoes and a
longer toe. But with very few exceptions this use of a heavier shoe
has done no great disservice to the breed at all. Indeed it has been
the brilliant animation of the Morgan in the show ring that has made
him so increasingly popular in recent years. His appeal in the ring is
a direct result of his distinctive beauty, and without it—with disappointing not-quite-high-enough action—he would not have risen to
the height he now enjoys. To be sure, there will always be a big demand for Morgan pleasure horses; but it has been his success in the
show ring that has made him known to the general public and subsequently put him in even greater demand. Showing is the best advertisement of any breed. The fact that many Morgans have made
such names for themselves in this field has had much to do with the
tremendous interest in them now.

SHOW TROT

Many owners and professional trainers of Morgans feel that the criticism over heavier shoes and longer toes by the pleasure-horse camp has been greatly exaggerated. Their accusations are for the most part ill-founded and unfair and have succeeded in doing nothing more than kindle the fires of battle among Morgan people.

A horse doesn't become an outstanding performance horse just by the growth of a longer toe or being shod with a weighted shoe. The ability must be there to begin with. It has been the mistaken idea among the uninitiated that the addition of these things will miraculously turn a pleasure horse into a show-ring champion. If any criticizing is to be done it should be dealt to those who misuse the weighted shoe in this unrealistic way, not directed to the conscientious horseman who through training and careful shoeing enhances the action of a Morgan that has show qualifications from the start. Often the weighted shoes are used only to balance the action of the horse that is high-going naturally.

There will always be a difference in the way a pleasure Morgan moves and the way a show Morgan handles himself; and, despite protests, this is as it should be. That the Morgan's way of going is distinctive from other breeds is an established fact, but it should also be an accepted fact that some Morgans are always going to have higher, showier action than others. And there are always going to be horsemen who will wish to enhance the action of this high-going Morgan through training and shoeing. These practices will scarcely "ruin" the breed as the pleasure-horse people would have us believe. So long as we stick to Morgan type in our breeding programs and strive for action, if it is desired, by breeding to strains which possess it, how can harm come to the Morgan breed as a whole? And if weighted shoes and a little longer toe will just put on the finishing touches—why not?

CANTER

THE CANTER: The slow, collected canter is the most desirable in the Morgan horse. It should be easy and smooth with no tendency to bunch up or move sideways. It should be relaxed and even, in the show ring as well as on the trail.

Any variations should be a matter of training for a specific purpose, such as working stock, cutting, etc.

To sum up action, then: the Morgan's way of going is all his own. His walk is rapid and energetic. His trot is, in the pleasure horse, easy and ground-covering with a characteristic briskness; in the show or performance it should be *naturally* high and brilliant and collected and balanced; the canter in both the pleasure horse and the show horse should be smooth, relaxed and straight on both leads.

VII

Influence on
Other American Breeds

FOR the admirers of the American Saddlebred horse the credit for establishing their breed belongs at the feet of its recognized foundation sire, the immortal Denmark. The Standardbred enthusiast reveres Imported Messenger as the patriarch of the Trotting Horse; and Allan F-1 has gone down in history as the foundation sire of the Tennessee Walking Horse.

Yet many are unaware of the fact that all three breeds share a common blood: that of the Morgan. Supporters of the Saddlebred and the Standardbred and the Walking Horse should pause and contemplate the contribution of the Morgan to each breed's success, for the thread of Morgan blood is woven inextricably through the pedigrees of their greatest stars.

THE AMERICAN SADDLEBRED

The Saddlebred originated in Kentucky early in that state's history. A need for horses for light harness and saddle work resulted in breeders developing a type of easy-gaited animal, which, while it had the stamina and hardiness needed for a raw new land, also possessed the quality and refinement so sought after by the avid horseman. This utility saddle horse of early Kentucky soon emerged as the forerunner of what we now know as the American Saddlebred.

Thoroughbred blood was brought in and crossed on native saddle-

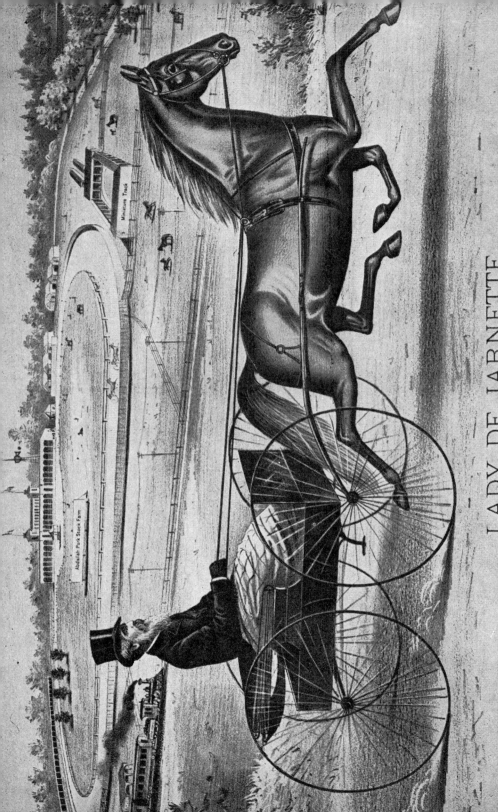

LADY DE JARNETTE.

THE HANDSOMEST EXHIBITION HORSE IN AMERICA.

type mares to give an increase in size and a generous measure of refinement and quality as well. Perhaps the most influential of the Thoroughbred importations to Kentucky was the seal-brown stallion Denmark, who had been foaled in 1839. Denmark was an extremely beautiful horse, although he had a racing record that was far from sensational, and it was soon discovered that his progeny were outstanding in the quality and beauty of their sire as well as in having the stamina so important to the times.

Denmark's best son was Gaines Denmark, whose dam was the Cockspur pacing mare known as "the Stevenson mare." A magnificent black stallion and a show horse of remarkable ability, Gaines Denmark became the founder of the Denmark strain of Saddle Horses. Through his four best-known sons—Washington's Denmark, Diamond Denmark, Star Denmark and Sumpter Denmark—the blood of Gaines Denmark had a profound effect on the advancement of the Saddlebred.

Then in 1863 there was foaled a Morgan-bred stallion, CABELL'S LEXINGTON, which was also destined to have a strong influence on the new breed being developed in Kentucky. Named on the original list of seventeen foundation sires of the *American Saddle Horse Register,* Cabell's Lexington remained on that list through two subsequent revisions and was only dropped, as were all the others, when in 1908 the National Saddle Horse Breeders Association voted to make Denmark the sole foundation sire of the breed. Another Morgan-bred stallion, COLEMAN'S EUREKA, was also retained on the list until it was decided to designate Denmark alone as the fountainhead of the breed.

Cabell's Lexington was sired by the little-known son of BLOOD'S BLACK HAWK called GIST'S BLACK HAWK. His dam was a good road mare by TOM HAL, a son of GREEN MOUNTAIN BLACK HAWK (also known as Sorrel Tom) a show horse and trotting stallion. Her dam was by Copperbottom (a Canadian pacer). The Canadian pacers were introduced into Kentucky around 1816 and the most famous of them were the original Tom Hal (according to Volume I of the Morgan *Register* no relation to the Tom Hal above) and Copperbottom. Old Tom Hal was noted for his toughness and endurance; he is said quite possibly to have been of Morgan blood, as there were horses of this breeding in that area of Canada where he was foaled. The blood of both Tom Hal and Copperbottom was influential in the establishment of the pacing strains in the Standardbred breed as well as having its effect on the Tennessee Walking Horse. Both stallions were natural pacers and although a great many others found their way into Kentucky and Tennessee, these two were the most famous of those horses known in the 1800s as the Canadian Pacers.

Cabell's Lexington, a dark bay with a star and three white socks, stood 15.2 and weighed 1,070 pounds. He had the beautiful head and the tiny ears of the Morgan, and was strong and compact of body with excellent legs and feet. During a long and very successful career in the show ring, Cabell's Lexington was beaten only once. And as a progenitor of outstanding saddle horses of the day, he had but one rival—Gaines Denmark. His get were noted for their fine dispositions and wonderful balanced action: traits which their sire had in abundance. They brought high prices and were in tremendous demand wherever there was an appreciation of fine horseflesh. The daughters of Cabell's Lexington, when crossed with such illustrious sires as Bourbon Chief and the great Harrison Chief, were responsible for many outstanding individuals of the Saddle Horse breed. Lexington's greatest son was Tom Boyd, a show horse of great brilliance and endurance (the latter being a trait often found lacking in today's show-ring performers—many a good horse is found to "run out of gas" nowadays when the workouts get too lengthy!). Cabell's Lexington himself had proved in his many successful onslaughts of the show ring that not only must a show horse have presence and action but, in the days when individual classes had fifty or more entries, it was necessary also that he have plenty of bottom and heart—plus a generous measure of the will to win. Some authorities state that old Lexington probably sired more fine saddle horses than any other sire of Morgan breeding. Certainly he was responsible for much of the greatness in several lines of American Saddlebred families.

Rivaling Cabell's Lexington in prominence as a Morgan-bred progenitor of Saddle Horses was another stallion whose name, as mentioned earlier, appeared on the original list of foundation sires of the Saddlebred. This was the dark chestnut COLEMAN'S EUREKA. Although his dam, Mary Boston, was of Thoroughbred blood tracing to the great Sir Archy, and bred for the race track, she also was a great success in the show ring before she was retired to the breeding farm. None can deny, however, that notwithstanding her showring record, her most significant contribution to the horse world, particularly that of the Saddle Horse, was her son Coleman's Eureka. Foaled in 1868 in Trimble County, Kentucky, Eureka was by YOUNG'S MORGAN, a grandson of BUTLER'S EUREKA. Butler's Eureka was by the celebrated Hale's Green Mountain Morgan and so was of the recognized Morgan type. In the words of the Morgan *Register,* Volume I, he was "as nice a chestnut horse as ever you saw, 15 hands, 1,000 pounds; very stylish . . ." His best sons were the sire of Young's Morgan and Cox's EUREKA—both sires of some of the finest horses in Frankfort County, Kentucky.

JUBILEE DE JARNETTE

Coleman's Eureka was 16 hands at maturity and a rich dark chestnut in color. He had a remarkable record in the show ring against the stiffest competition that section of the country had to offer. In 1877 he won a first premium at St. Louis, Missouri, with forty-two competitors. The *National Saddle Horse Register* says, "Coleman's Eureka was a horse of remarkable power to transmit his good qualities, and Kentucky is full of good stallions and mares that trace to him. Some of the finest saddle horses of the present time have much of his blood. . . ." Through his daughters, his blood flows in the veins of such great show horses as King Bourbon, Chester Chief and the stallion American Born. But the blood of Coleman's Eureka, while it is found in abundance in the Saddlebred, has been lost to the Morgan through absorption into the former.

INDIAN CHIEF, by Blood's Black Hawk, a son of old Black Hawk 20, was another Morgan stallion who left his mark indelibly on the American Saddlebred. Foaled in 1858 in Cynthiana, Kentucky, he was kept most of his life in Harrison County, near Cynthiana. His sire, Blood's Black Hawk, was foaled in Wells River, Vermont, in 1847 and taken to Lexington, Kentucky, by a man named Blood, his breeder, in 1853. He won a first premium at the Kentucky State Fair in 1856 and was shown in harness singly and double, gaining himself a sizable record of wins. The dam of Indian Chief was Lou Berry who was by Ned Forrest, he by Young Bashaw. She traced to Thoroughbred blood through both her sire and dam. Indian Chief was a bay horse with a stripe and a left hind stocking. He stood 16 hands and weighed 1,100 pounds. He had a lively patronage throughout his life, for he was not only a successful sire of "fine-styled roadsters and fancy drivers" but himself a show horse of distinction. B. J. Treacy, a prominent Kentucky breeder of the time, said of Indian Chief, "He was, in his day, one of the most beautiful horses that ever lived and almost invincible in the show ring." He won the Champion Sweepstakes at the St. Louis Fair in 1878; and there were sixty-three entries in the class!

However many feel that the siring of the incomparable LADY DE JARNETTE was his greatest claim to fame, for she was the undisputed champion of show rings the country over. One of the brightest stars

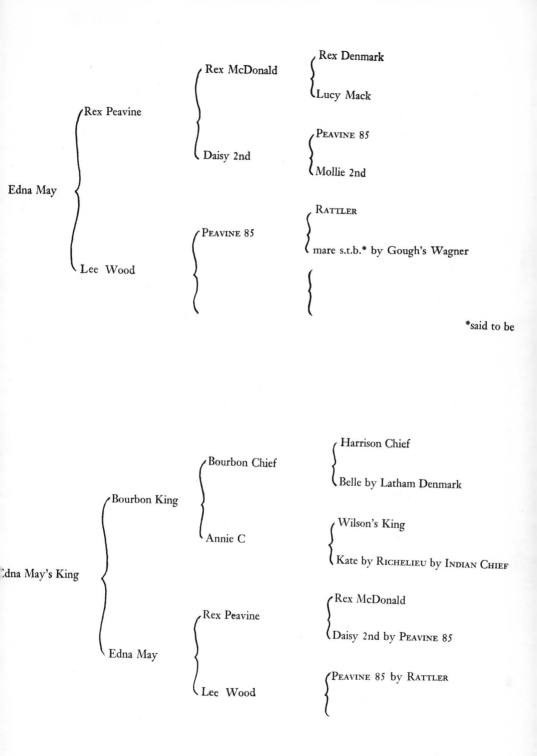

Edna May
- Rex Peavine
  - Rex McDonald
    - Rex Denmark
    - Lucy Mack
  - Daisy 2nd
    - Peavine 85
    - Mollie 2nd
- Lee Wood
  - Peavine 85
    - Rattler
    - mare s.t.b.* by Gough's Wagner

*said to be

Edna May's King
- Bourbon King
  - Bourbon Chief
    - Harrison Chief
    - Belle by Latham Denmark
  - Annie C
    - Wilson's King
    - Kate by Richelieu by Indian Chief
- Edna May
  - Rex Peavine
    - Rex McDonald
    - Daisy 2nd by Peavine 85
  - Lee Wood
    - Peavine 85 by Rattler

of that or any era, the Lady remained undefeated throughout her career, and was called on numerous occasions the most perfect harness show mare of all time. Since none of her contemporaries could even approach her performance, she was finally barred from competition in the ring. Thereafter her life in the limelight consisted of exhibitions at horse shows and fairs where $500 a week was paid for her appearances. After her show-ring career was over, the Lady was sold for $5,000 to a gentleman in Boston who kept her until her death. Lady de Jarnette's only colt was the stallion JUBILEE DE JARNETTE, a son of JUBILEE LAMBERT, by Daniel Lambert. This stallion, sold to J. C. Brunk of Springfield, Illinois, was used on Morgan mares; thereby returning the blood of Indian Chief to this breed.

But except through his daughter, Lady de Jarnette, the blood of Indian Chief was responsible for greatness in the American Saddlebred instead of the Morgan, for like Cabell's Lexington and Coleman's Eureka he was destined to become one of the outstanding foundation sires of the Saddlebred. Like the others, too, his daughters were important broodmares, for when bred to such great stallions as Bourbon Chief and Harrison Chief, they produced show horses of outstanding ability.

Indian Chief also got the brown stallion RICHELIEU, who was the sire of Kate, the dam of Annie C. Since Annie C was the dam of three of the Saddle breed's greatest stallions—Bourbon King, Montgomery Chief and Marvel King—she was voted one of the most eminent broodmares of all time. Bourbon King was considered among the horsemen of his day to be above reproach. In the show ring and as a sire he won the wildest acclaim. He was never defeated under saddle wherever he was shown even though his competition was the top show horses of his day. Bourbon King in turn sired yet another great show horse and family-builder with a nearly unequaled record in the breed, the remarkable Edna May's King. Out of Edna May, who traced to Morgan ancestry through both her sire *and* her dam, this famous stallion got Anacacho Shamrock (sire of Wing Commander), Anacacho Denmark and Cameo Kirby. Also by Bourbon King was the magnificent show stallion King's Genius, who undoubtedly has worn out just as many superlatives as his illustrious sire and grandsire! He was the finest example of the Rex Peavine-Bourbon King cross and became still another sire of a great line.

Now, of all the Morgan names in the Saddle breed, none is more familiar to those of us who admire Morgans than PEAVINE. The name had its origin in PEAVINE 85, a registered Morgan stallion foaled in Kentucky in 1863. Peavine was by RATTLER, who was by STOCKBRIDGE CHIEF, a son of Black Hawk 20. A chestnut with a very heavy mane and tail, he stood 16 hands and weighed 1,150. A show horse in his own right, Peavine got a great many fine horses in his home country. He was also a harness-race horse and had a mark of 2:35½. Peavine sired Daisy 2nd, the dam of Rex Peavine, and this alone assured him a place in Saddle Horse annals. He also sired the dam of Edna May, whose pedigree and that of her son, Edna May's King, give a fair example of how Morgan blood has assisted in the production of outstanding Saddlebreds.

All the above-mentioned stallions of Morgan blood and innumerable others—as well as many, many unrecorded mares—have been of untold value in the development of the American Saddle Horse. Both of the two most well-known families of the breed—the Chiefs and the Denmarks—have felt the Morgan influence. Especially through the Chiefs and Peavines has the blood of the Morgan had its greatest effect. These families are noted for their substance, style and brilliant action.

It is interesting to the Morgan enthusiast to note that of the 11,977 horses registered in the first four volumes of the *American Saddle Horse Register,* horses tracing in male line to Justin Morgan number 714, or 6 percent of the total registered. And included in this number are some of the most venerated stars of the breed.

THE STANDARDBRED HORSE

Until the advent of Hambletonian 10 (Rysdyk's), foaled in 1849, the Morgan horse was the king of the road and the race track. Black Hawk and his descendants were *the* harness-race horses standing in undisputed favor throughout the racing world in the early nineteenth century. Gradually, however, the decendants of a gray English Thoroughbred named Messenger began appearing on the scene to

WALKER MORRILL

steal some of the Morgans' thunder. Messenger, imported from England in 1788, traced to all three of the Eastern stallions which were
the foundation sires of the Thoroughbred: the Darley Arabian, the
Byerly Turk and the Godolphin Arabian. Like Denmark in the
Saddlebred *Register,* Messenger became the foundation sire of a new
breed, for he was recognized as the founding father of the American
Trotter. Although he was a horse bred and trained for the running
gait, Messenger sired horses with a peculiar proclivity for the trot.
His offspring—sons and especially grandsons—were soon to whittle
away at the stronghold of the Morgan, chalking up records that even
the most pro-Morgan horsemen could not fail to recognize. Ethan
Allan 50, the darling of New England and a racing crack who was
admired wherever he appeared, was the last of the great Morgan
stars; his retirement became the swan song of the full-blooded Morgan's supremacy on the track. Little by little the larger, faster Messengers, and subsequently the Hambletonians, drove the Morgans to

the wall as far as racing was concerned. But not before the influence of the Morgan breed had left its indelible mark.

A prominent Morgan family to influence the new breed—eventually to be known as the Standardbred—were the Morrills, a line descending from Bulrush, as we have noted in Chapter V. The patriarch of the family was Old Morrill; his best son, Perkins' Young Morrill, carried the line on. Outstanding among the descendants of Old Morrill were Winthrop Morrill, sire of twenty-seven winners and founder of a great strain of trotters, and Fearnaught (2:23¼), one-time Champion Trotting Stallion and head of a trotting family second only to the Ethan Allens for speed. Winthrop Morrill, though bred to the plainest, run-of-the-mill mares, sired a great many speedy trotters and despite the handicap of common mares stood fifth on the

GOLDDUST

NIGHTSHADE dam a well bred Virginia mare

SUPERB by Ethan Allen, dam by Harris Hambletonian

BLACK DIAMOND dam by Vermont Black Hawk

BLACK ETHAN ALLEN, dam by Old Washington, he by Mambrino Paymaster

THE CELEBRATED FOUR IN HAND STALLION TEAM

list of sires of 2:30 performers in 1877. Fearnaught, his half-brother, was a popular race horse and an equally popular sire and frequent prize-winner in the show ring. He had a number of owners, one of whom was reported to have paid $25,000 to possess him.

Draco, another grandson of Old Morrill, and his brother, Danville Boy, were two more Morgan stallions who, after successful careers on the track, forged still more Morgan links in the chain of the Standardbred family through sons and daughters bred for the track.

WALKER MORRILL, a son of Winthrop Morrill, was yet another prominent sire of Morgan blood. Foaled in 1861, he sired six known 2:30 trotters and was the winner of thirty-six races himself. And so it went: a list of the descendants of Old Morrill alone and the growing number of "two-thirty" horses would fill a volume.

But there were other lines and individuals that had their season of fame before being swallowed up by the Hambletonians.

One such individual was GOLDDUST. From his description it would seem he had been rightly named, for he was said to have been "pure gold in color." Foaled in 1855, Golddust was the son of VERMONT MORGAN by BARNARD MORGAN, a son of Old Gifford. His dam was the Hoke mare, who was said to have been sired by Zilcaadi, a chestnut Arabian stallion which had been the gift of the Sultan of Morocco to the U.S. Consul, Mr. Rhind, who imported him.

Golddust was a stallion of extreme beauty; yet beauty alone did not win him the esteem and popularity accorded him all his life. He had a brilliant career although the short span of sixteen years marked his lifetime.

Foaled the property of Andrew Hoke near Louisville, Kentucky, Golddust was sold as a weanling to L. L. Dorsey. He remained at Dorsey's Eden Stock Farm all his life, so fond was that gentleman of his golden stallion. Golddust was a large horse by Morgan standards, standing 16 hands and weighing 1,275 pounds. To quote Volume I of the Morgan *Register*: "Golddust was a most beautiful horse, and one of the very great sires of the country. In getting extreme speed he outranks Hambletonian, only three of whose more than 1,300 colts are found in the 2:20 list, the best of which is Dexter with a record of 2:17½ made against time."

Draco

In his brief lifetime Golddust sired 302 foals, yet two made the 2:20 list. His greatest offspring was LUCILLE GOLDDUST, who had a record of 2:16½, which she made in a hotly contested race.

The Civil War years and the ensuing turmoil caused by them, resulted in Golddust having fewer opportunities at stud than a less unstable situation might have offered. That, coupled with his all-too-early demise, put a limit to his successes. Nevertheless his place is assured and he stands strong on his accomplishments despite the adversities life meted out to him. He sired thirty-eight winners, and among his sons sixteen became outstanding sires in their own right.

Ethan Allen 50, whose story is found earlier in this book, was probably the most prolific of the Morgans in regard to production of outstanding harness horses. His line overshadows all others and, unlike some of the others, his contribution to the Morgan breed was as consequential as the legacy he left to the American Trotter. Ethan Allen

ROBERT WILKES!

Dark Grey Stallion, Foaled May 10, 1885. Sire, Mambrino Wilkes, Record 2.28¾

Sire of Arthur Wilkes, 2.24¼, R. M. Wilkes, 2.27¼, by George Wilkes, 2.22, sire of Harry Wilkes, 2.13½, Guy Wilkes, 2.15¼, Mike Wilkes, 2.14½, Wilcox, 2.16½, Wilson, 2.16½, So So, 2.17½, J. B. Richardson, 2.17¼, Baron Wilkes, 2.18, Bud Crook, 2.18½, Rosa Wilkes, 2.18½, and fifty-five other 2.30 performers, dam, Lady Gilmore, by Honest Allen, sire of four in the 2.30 list, by Ethan Allen, 2.25½, sire of seven 2.30 trotters, of eighteen sons that have sired seventy trotters, and of fourteen dams that have produced fifteen trotters.

ROBERT WILKES is a horse of beautiful conformation, stands 15½ hands high, and weighs 1,025 pounds. Through his sire he gets the blood of

Hambletonian, Henry Clay, and Mambrino Chief

The three leading strains of blood in the trotter, and through his dam comes New England's favorite blood, the Morgan. Lady Gilmore was a fast and spirited roadster, of unflinching courage and great endurance, and in her five-year-old form was sold for $800. By right of inheritance ROBERT WILKES should be a trotter and a sire of trotters; and he certainly is the

BEST BRED WILKES AND MORGAN STALLION

Standing for service in the State of Vermont. His sire, Mambrino Wilkes, placed two in the list last year, and will add several more this season. Both Arthur Wilkes, 2.24¼, and R. M. Wilkes, 2.27¼, that got records last season, are expected to trot in 2.20 or better this year. Of George Wilkes, the grandsire of Robert Wilkes, it is simply necessary to state that the records show him to be the greatest sire of trotters and campaigners the world has ever known. No less than forty-one of his grandsons and granddaughters entered the magic circle during the year 1888.

ROBERT WILKES

Will serve a limited number of approved mares during the season of 1889, at my Stable near my Blacksmith Shop, for

$20, TO WARRANT

If you have a good mare to breed from, don't fail to examine this royally bred and elegant young Stallion.

HENRY S. NEWTON

WEST RANDOLPH, Vt.

SPECIAL ANNOUNCEMENT.

I, the owner of the stallion Robert Wilkes, which horse is kept in Randolph, Vt., hereby declare my intention to take advantage of an Act for the protection of horse owners, No. 104 of the Acts and Resolves of the General Assembly of Vermont, at the tenth biennial session, 1888.

sired seventy winners and was the winner, himself, of over thirty races against some of the top names of his day. His greatest sons were, in addition to Daniel Lambert, DeLong's ETHAN ALLEN, HOLABIRD'S ETHAN ALLEN, AMERICAN ETHAN, SUPERB, WOODWARD'S ETHAN ALLEN and HONEST ALLEN.

Honest Allen, foaled in 1855, got DENNING ALLEN, who was the sire of LORD CLINTON, a black gelding who had a laudable race record and a mark of 2:10¼! Denning Allen was triumphant in the show ring, winning First Premium for Morgan Stallions Five and Over, and Sweepstakes for Morgan Stallions, All Ages, at the World's Columbian Exposition in Chicago in 1893. His full brother, GENERAL GATES, stood at the head of the United States Morgan Horse Farm breeding program in Weybridge, Vermont.

Daniel Lambert, Ethan Allen's best son, filled his sire's shoes to overflowing, for he was another great speed sire and a prolific one as well. He got a goodly number of colts with Morgan beauty of line and movement and speed to boot (a combination which was often found to be lacking in the Hambletonians). His family included thirty-seven offspring with 2:30-or-better records, and one hundred six winners. Thirty-one of his sons became well-known sires, among them: ADDISON LAMBERT, ARISTOS, BEN FRANKLIN and COBDEN in addition to JUBILEE LAMBERT, and a host of others which wove the thread of Morgan blood intricately through that of the Hambletonian.

A stallion which probably technically could only be called half-Morgan, yet nevertheless traced to the blood of Justin Morgan, was Kentucky Prince. A bay stallion foaled in 1870, he was by Clark Chief (by Mambrino Chief, by Mambrino, by Imported Messenger). Prince was out of Kentucky Queen sired by MORGAN EAGLE, a son of Hale's Green Mountain. It might have been his breeding or his trotting ability or perhaps his sheer good looks: but at any rate, his name appears in more Trotting-horse pedigrees than that of any Morgan-bred stallion. Kentucky Prince sired winners of almost three hundred races, became the grandsire of about seventy-five more winners, and the great-grandsire of countless others. He was a half-brother to Harrison Chief, both being by Clark Chief. And while Harrison

Chief went on to fame in the annals of the American Saddlebred, Kentucky Prince will be remembered as a prominent sire in Trotting Horse history.

The names of Morgans woven in the tapestry of Standardbred greats is seemingly endless, and their numbers and their records if set down would surely make the reader's head swim. Suffice it is to say that although the Hambletonian blood has at last obscured all others today, still the heritage of those old Morgans will be there in the twentieth-century champions tracing to them. There are many trottingbred all-time greats which carry crosses to Justin Morgan. Among them are Lee Axworthy, Uhlan and Hamburg Belle. The champion trotter Greyhound (1:55¼) has five crosses to Justin Morgan, and Titan Hanover (2:00) has *no less than twenty-two* crosses to Justin. So be it. The Morgan rests its case.

THE TENNESSEE WALKING HORSE

Although not so great as on the Saddlebred and the Standardbred, nonetheless the influence of Morgan blood is felt on the Walking Horse through a little mare called MAGGIE MARSHALL, the dam of Allan F-1. Since the greatest number of horses entered in the first volume of the Walking Horse *Register* trace directly to him, Allan F-1 is called the fountainhead of the breed.

Allan F-1 was foaled in 1886 in Lexington, Kentucky. He was by Allandorf, a grandson of George Wilkes (George Wilkes, it will be remembered, was one of Hambletonian's best sons) and his top line contained the names of such greats in the trotting world as Mambrino Chief and Mambrino Patchen. But it is his Morgan dam we are interested in here. Maggie Marshall was by a good son of old Black Hawk named BRADFORD'S TELEGRAPH. Telegraph was called "one of Black Hawk's most stylish and fine-stepping colts." He was foaled in Monkton, Vermont, in 1849. He stood 15.3, weighed 1,100 pounds and was jet black with a star and white stockings behind. Descriptions of Telegraph indicate that he was a powerful horse with a tremendous amount of vitality. He had a good disposition and was quite typical of the best Morgans. He was speedy and possessed of remarkable endurance as well.

Telegraph was taken to Ohio in 1854 and subsequently arrived at Augusta, Kentucky, where he remained until his death in 1876. E. D. Herr of Lexington owned his daughter, Maggie Marshall, when she produced the foal Allan F-1 in 1886. Allan was sold, with Maggie his dam, to George F. Fly of Elyria, Ohio; but because of an inclination to pace during training, he failed to find favor with his owner who was more interested in trotters and cast a baleful eye upon the "side-wheeling" gait of the colt. Allan was returned to Kentucky and consigned to a sale there. The price, $355, landed him in Murfreesboro, Tennessee. But good fortune had not caught up with Allan yet. A failure as a harness horse, he was used as a breeding stallion, only to be a washout again. Then a series of degrading sales finally put him in the stables of James Brantley, who had done considerable investigating into the little black stallion's background.

Allan was a good-looking horse with a well-shaped head, a graceful neck and the symmetrical body and fine, strong legs inherited from his Morgan dam. His tendency to do the running walk convinced his newest owner that he had the necessary attributes for a sire of plantation saddle horses. His top walking mare, Gertrude, who through her dam traced to Gifford Morgan, seemed a likely individual to begin his breeding program; the following year, 1906, the mare produced Roan Allen F-38. A strawberry roan with a flaxen mane and tail, a broad blaze and white stockings behind, Roan Allen was a striking horse in all respects. Those who remember the horse say his gait was faultless: speedy and smooth with the characteristic gliding stride which was so pleasurable to his rider. They said he carried himself proudly, with his long tail streaming behind him and his head erect. Roan Allen was much admired all his life and there was just reason why he should become one of the most celebrated Walking Horse foundation sires.

Although the nucleus of the Walking Horse breed had begun forming long before the appearance of Allan F-1 and his son Roan Allen, these two launched it officially, as Hambletonian had launched the American Trotter. Old Allan F-1 died in 1910 at twenty-four years of age but another breed, strengthened by the blood of the *first* American breed, the Morgan, was established and on its way.

VIII

In the Show Ring

FROM early times Morgans have been no strangers to the applause of the show ring. Their natural, high-headed carriage and characteristic presence lend themselves to exhibition perhaps as much as the bred-for-the-ring showiness of the American Saddlebred. Even back in the days of Old Gifford and his famous son, Hale's Green Mountain Morgan, it has been the Morgan horse that has commanded the scene on so many occasions. Old Gifford even at the advanced age of twenty-three drew cheers from the crowd at the New York State Fair held in Saratoga in 1847 as he was paraded in front of the grandstand with a cavalcade of his fine sons and daughters behind him. And Green Mountain Morgan won championship after championship at state fairs from Vermont to Michigan to Ohio in 1853, and as a result breeders from wherever he was shown poured into New England seeking Morgans for use in their breeding programs.

Black Hawk, one of the best-known Morgans of his time, took by storm the first Vermont State Fair held in Middlebury in 1851. With seventy-five of his sons and daughters, he was a magnificent sight when ridden by his owner at the head of this excellent group. There was, at the time, a lively rivalry between Black Hawk and Hale's Green Mountain Morgan in the show ring, a competition manifested by the great gathering of the best-of-the-get of each stallion at the state fair in Rutland, Vermont, in 1852. This was reportedly one of the best showings of Morgans ever seen.

Each succeeding year at state fairs and other livestock expositions, whenever they were shown, the Morgans always went away with the

sound of applause in their ears. Exhibited usually in hand or in harness, their beauty and manners always left the very best impression, and a huge demand for them was created as a result of such favorable showings. As mentioned earlier, they were unexcelled roadsters and their popularity in this field never diminished until the advent of the automobile. Their heyday on the race track reached its culmination with Ethan Allen and, before they were swept from that field of endeavor by the Hambletonians and early Standardbreds, they made history on the tracks of America.

And so it would seem that the show ring with its attendant glamor is as natural a setting for the Morgan as were the race track, a side-hill farm or the Post Road to Boston. His heritage is deeply rooted in all of them, and although today his use on the road in harness is practically nil (except occasionally for pleasure driving in rural areas) and the old horse rake and the sulky plow are rusting in the wagon shed, he may still command attention in the show rings of *this* age. Here, as in days long past, he may feel the admiring eyes upon him and hear the swell of applause as his ancestors heard it a hundred years ago.

FIRST IMPRESSIONS

Not since the days of the great Vermont State Fairs with their huge gathering of old-time Morgans has the breed enjoyed the popularity and prestige in the show ring it does today. From the low ebb of the '30s through the increasing enthusiasm of the '40s, the Morgan once again has atttained the position in the show ring that he had before World War I. More and more, the breeders of Morgans are realizing the function as well as the fun of showing their horses. As evidenced by the great annual classic, the National Morgan Horse Show, interest in the breed has increased tremendously through the publicity and promotion of the Morgan through this and other all-Morgan events. Horse shows put the different breeds of horses on display for the horse-loving public and potential buyers. They are a showcase, as it were, where newcomers can see all breeds at their best and evaluate and choose the qualities they most want in the horse they may wish to own.

Morgans, with their wonderful versatility, are ever widening their field of admirers, and not since their heyday as trotting cracks and roadsters have they enjoyed such popularity as they do in this age of the atom and the missile. And the Morgan is back on solid footing, too, for a horse of the Morgan's versatility and type is in great demand: as a family horse, an all-round pleasure horse, and, as will be discussed here, a show horse of outstanding ability.

My own introduction to the Morgan took place at a horse show. It was here that I had my first impression of the breed—and that impression has remained with me always. 'Way back in my mind I have the picture of the Morgans as I saw them in the ring for the first time. Having read about Morgans and heard about them, I was most anxious actually to see them in the flesh and the impression they made upon me at the time, I remember, was that here was the horse I had always wanted; here was all the symmetry and spirit which delights an artist's eye, and with it the controlled vigor to please the

rider. Then and there, it was the Morgan for me! I had seen all kinds of horses before—beautiful individuals of many breeds—but there was always something lacking in all of them. And whatever that illusive something was, I found it at last in the Morgan.

The class was the Championship Saddle Stake and it was so long ago I don't remember the names of the horses or their bloodlines; but I do remember there were two stallions in the class that literally took my breath away when they entered the ring. It was an indoor arena and the lighting was good. And suddenly for me there was nothing else to be noticed but these two Morgan stallions making their first trip around the ring at a trot. One was black, or so dark a chestnut that he appeared black; the other was a deep mahogany bay. Their lovely arched and crested necks, their fine heads with huge bright eyes sparkling, their bold, trappy trot impressed me more than all the lofty Saddlebreds I had ever seen. The stallions were all show horse—and yet there was something more. That sparkling spirit that is a part of their outlook, that inherent, eager, proud, "look-at-me, I'm-tops" expression about them that to me is purely Morgan. I don't recall the winner of the class—they were both equally deserving—but it doesn't matter. All I remember was that a shutter clicked and I had a picture in my mind of the Morgan horse, one I shall always remember. . . .

Because of this experience I am of the opinion that the show ring is the best place for first impressions. My reasons are these: (1) the novice sees the horses under the best possible circumstances; (2) usually the individuals shown are for the most part the better examples of the breed, and (3) quite often at a breeding farm animals are apt to be "in the rough" (understandably so) and it is difficult for the newcomer to visualize how an animal will look in top condition if, for example, it has hair a mile long on its fetlocks and has been availing itself of a mud bath in the corner of the pasture—first impressions, you know!

THE EARLY NATIONALS

The National Morgan Horse Show has been exceedingly instrumental in promotion of the breed. First held in 1939 to celebrate the

150th anniversary of the birth of Justin Morgan, "the National," as it is affectionately known, is a horse show, old-home week and a great gathering-of-the-clans, all rolled into those hectic, wouldn't-miss-it-for-the-world days. The spirit and enthusiasm which have prevailed at all Nationals since '39 is an indication of the wonderful camaraderie that exists among Morgan people. From the time the first van or trailer has rolled onto the grounds, the atmosphere is one of friendliness and excited anticipation. No matter whether or not everyone may agree on the best type of present-day Morgan, no more than two persons are needed to start a lively discussion on the favorite subject—MORGANS!

The seeds of the National were sown in the small showings of Morgans held at the finish of the annual 100-Mile Trail Rides which were sponsored by The Green Mountain Horse Association in Woodstock, Vermont. The Morgan show was begun in order to bring Morgans into the limelight and thereby advance and promote the breed. The shows were cosponsored by The Green Mountain Horse Association and The Morgan Horse Club.

The 1939 National Morgan Horse Show was held at Owen Moon's Upwey Farm in South Woodstock, Vermont, and conducted under the guidance of Mr. Moon. Like the previous shows the '39 National was held following the completion of the 100-Mile Trail Ride. Fifteen classes were crowded into the half-day show.

From 1939 to 1942 South Woodstock was the scene of the National, and it was becoming an eagerly anticipated yearly event when the Second World War terminated it until 1947. That year—'47—Mr. Moon, whose tremendous interest and support had helped the Morgan show to its success, passed away. He was sorely missed, as so many of the "horse projects" in and around Woodstock had had their first impetus from him.

The 1947 show, the first National since the war, was held that year in Windsor, Vermont, at the farm of Mr. and Mrs. F. O. Davis, called Wind-Crest. Situated on a hilltop above the busy town of Windsor, with a perfect panoramic view of the surrounding Vermont countryside, Wind-Crest was a lovely setting for the successful show held there that year. In 1948 and '49 Wind-Crest again provided the facilities and the hospitality for the National before the show was moved to a new location in Windsor for the 1950 event. The new setting was on the banks of the Connecticut River where Buena Vista Farm was National host for the years 1950 and 1951.

In 1952 the National was moved once again. Feeling that a more central location would draw an even greater number of entries than in previous years, the committee voted to hold the '52 National at Northampton, Massachusetts. Held at the Tri-County Fairgrounds, the facilities were conducive to a greater number of entries. The racing sheds provided abundant stabling and the track, large show ring and grandstand were definite assets considering the growing number of people who planned to show at the National each year. As compared with the fifteen classes and few dozen entries at the first National at Woodstock, the 1952 show boasted fifty-one classes and over one hundred Morgans on the grounds. The show was a huge success with great spectator appeal throughout the variety of interesting classes.

Best Feet Forward

Each year found a growing number of Morgans exhibited. And not only were they increasing in numbers but, evident to all, was the better uniformity among the horses presented to the judges. Also in evidence was a certain professional air in the way they were handled and shown.

In the 1930s and the early '40s the Morgan was often shown in the ring with mane roached and tail trimmed. Competing with the American Saddlebred and other breeds on equal footing, many Morgans, by their animation and presence, were frequent winners in Open Saddle Classes. But many breeders, feeling that the Morgan might become absorbed into Saddlehorse type, demanded that the Morgan club instigate a set of rules governing the Morgan in the show ring. Until the 1953 show season the Morgan was permitted to wear quarter boots and ribbons in the style of the Saddlebred. Hoping to pull away permanently from the Saddlebred influence, The Morgan Horse Club made a rule whereby no artificial appliances like the quarter boot could be used on the Morgan in the show ring.

". . . no more braids 'n boots."

Many felt that this would curtail some of the practices which they considered disagreeable to the breed.

But despite efforts to keep the Morgan completely natural—and even a mite backwoodsy—the breed has progressed to the point where, at least in the show ring, it has attained that certain amount of polish which is essential in the promotion of any product—whether it be a horse, an automobile or a basket of apples! For example, the period of showing Morgans in harness in old Bailey buggies is ended now, with the shiny fine-harness show buggy taking their place. Very few are the Morgans who now come to the National with long fetlocks and a fringe of hair under their jaws. Trimmed ears and muzzles, polished hoofs, clean and wavy luxurious manes and tails, and gleaming tack correctly appointed—all are becoming more and more in evidence. The days seem to be gone when Morgans were likely to be exhibited right from the pasture, as it were. This is as it should be: a consciousness of the fact that fitting and showmanship sometimes make or break a good horse. Much of the newly acquired professionalism has made for a great gain in prestige from ringside observers.

Some of the classes which fascinate spectators and show them just what a Morgan can do include: the Justin Morgan Performance Class, where the horses are raced a half-mile in harness, then run a half-mile under saddle, then shown in the ring at a walk, trot, and canter, and lastly, under work harness, they are asked to pull a stone-boat with 1,000 pounds added; the Versatility Class requires them to work in harness, under saddle and to jump two obstacles; the Roadsters Under Saddle and the Roadsters in Harness require speed at the trot and are shown in the ring; and probably the most exciting of all are the two races on the track—the Half-Mile Race in harness

Final thrill in a Justin Morgan Performance Class.

GEORGE GOBEL *showing classic Morgan speed.*   Patriquin

and the Half-Mile Race under saddle at the trot. There are also a class for Morgan jumpers and another one for Morgan working stock horses.

The following is an example which might serve to illustrate how a bit of professional quick thinking and showmanship made all the difference in how a class of Morgans was judged and pinned.

A friend of mine was to show a mare in a Model Morgan Class at a comparatively important horse show in Vermont. The mare was of above-average type and conformation and was at the time in excellent condition and turned out properly, but she had a head that, while good, lacked a certain amount of expression. My friend knew he had his work cut out for him as the mare was to compete against stallions as well as other mares and geldings. Being a showman by nature, he waited outside the gate until all the other entries were in the ring and then, popping the whip he carried, alerted the mare and led her into the ring at a brisk, animated trot. Down the center of the ring he ran with the mare really tramping beside him. The judge, hearing the hoofbeats behind him, turned and immediately focused all his attention on the mare. He watched her trot squarely by him, come to a halt and, at a word from my friend, stretch out into a perfect pose. Then he turned to judge the entries at the other end of the line. Needless to say, however, he had my friend's mare already carefully considered.

Now it happened that there was one stallion in this class that was thought by many to be an excellent individual and was considered the horse to beat. But he fidgeted and would not stand still. As the judge made his way down the line of entries, my friend's mare, becoming a bit bored by the inactivity, lost some of the alertness she had had upon entering the ring; and, as a model horse is required to have expression as well as type and conformation, my friend was frankly worried. But he handled the situation to perfection. At the moment the judge turned toward the mare to look her over, he shook the bit a little and taking off his hat he pushed it toward the mare's nose, at the same time making a whooshing noise through his teeth. The mare, not frightened but suddenly awakened, put up her head, arched her neck and pricked her ears sharply. Her eyes, glued to my friend's hat, sparkled with interest. This is the picture she made to the judge as he looked her over. It did not take him long to mark his card and turn it in. When the results were called over the PA system there were about four stallion owners who had very red faces: wonder of wonders, the little chestnut mare had bettered them all—even the horse to beat!

Many of the railbirds, including myself, knew we had witnessed about as pure an example of showmanship as we would see in many a day—and it takes a huge amount of it to win with a mare in a field of stallions.

The Golden Mean

While some people felt that too much professionalism was bad for Morgans, there were just as many coming to realize that much had been done for the Morgan in the show ring by professional trainers. However as any extreme is neither desirable nor to be tolerated for long, criticism soon arose over some of the practices used by a few of the trainers to get results with the Morgans in their care. Possibly this initiated the continuous loud protests over whips and spurs and long feet and heavy shoes and shackles and the whole gamut of appliances which supposedly make the Saddlebred "climb." "Not for Morgans!" was the cry; "we want 'em natural. We want NATURAL ACTION."

Then came the query—what's natural? For a Morgan? Who's to say? What one horse can do quite spontaneously another will need special training and shoeing to achieve (comparably, they're just like some children who learn ballet with no apparent effort while others require long hours of practice and related gymnastics).

It is pointless to condemn all users of show shoes just because a few are foolish enough to think that all it takes to make a performance horse is an exaggerated toe and a heavy shoe. This is ridiculous: there is a great deal more to a show horse than that.

IMPACT OF RECENT NATIONALS

From 1952 to the present time the National has been held at Northampton. And, as in previous years, an increasing number of Morgans appear each year. The 1960 National found over three hundred fifty horses entered in seventy-six classes. New stables were built between '53 and '59 until now there are more than enough stalls to accommodate the ever-growing number of entries.

With more than three hundred Morgans shown in '60, it can be readily imagined what a tremendous spectacle that the National has become. People interested in the breed visit the stable area and, finding Morgan folks exceedingly friendly and anxious to talk about their horses, learn much about Morgans and why they have become so popular. Although the show itself now lasts but four days, for some exhibitors—like those who attend with as many as fifteen or sixteen horses—it becomes a major operation; it is not unusual to have Morgans at the fairgrounds for up to two weeks or longer.

The publicity from the National alone has furthered the cause of the Morgan horse to an amazing degree. To use a show-business expression, everybody wants to get into the act. Anyway so it would seem, for never has the interest in and the demand for Morgans been so great as in the last five or six years. Throughout New England,

MADALIN winning Grand Champion Harness Stake at the 1??? American

New York and the Mid-Atlantic states the result of National show publicity is being felt with an increasing number of entries exhibiting from these areas. Even horses from as far away as Michigan, Illinois, and Kansas attended the '60 National, so important has the show become.

Not only at the National are the Morgans making their presence felt, but in many of the major horse shows in the East they are proving to be great crowd pleasers. Where once show committees were skeptical about offering a full division for the breed, they now are most anxious to have Morgans represented at their shows. In New England the Morgan classes often dominate the show. Thus no one can disagree that the great call for Morgans recently is from the excellent account of themselves they have made in the important shows.

Local affiliates of The Morgan Horse Club all over the country report a tremendous upsurge in the demand for registered Morgans and the parent club itself reports more activity now than at any time since its founding in 1909.

The Midwest also has its shows for Morgans, with the great Illinois State Fair being the highlight. Colorado and Washington State have held all-Morgan shows with successful results. And at each show the country over the Morgan makes new friends.

SHOWING AND MORGAN TYPES

It would seem, considering the success of the Morgan in the show ring, that all breeders—and in fact every person interested in the promotion of the breed—would be heartily in favor of Morgan show-ring activities. However there are unfortunately a few dissenters who still feel that the Morgan's place is on the trail and that the show Morgans are Morgans in name only.

This minority, and luckily it is a minority, object especially to, quote, "Those, high-going, Saddlebred types which are not typical Morgans." Unquote. This criticism is a grave injustice to those breeders who have, through selection and diligent training, produced Morgans that are born-and-bred show horses in every sense of the word and yet are still Morgan in type and conformation. They are not "Saddlebred," nor do they move like Saddlebreds, albeit they have a lofty carriage and can trot a level forearm. Without this ability they would have no appeal in the show ring; an appeal which has done more to interest show committees and spectators (potential buyers) than pleasure horses ever could, no matter how perfect.

In the show ring, the high, brilliant action is desirable: let's face it—do we want the spectators to go out to lunch when the Morgan classes are called into the ring because their appearance holds little more excitement than a road hack class, or do we want them to shout with delight as the Morgans trot around the ring with manes and tails streaming, legs flashing? A show horse *must* be showy! He must have the presence and animation to hold the interest of the gallery. This the Morgan can do. Why deprive him of the chance with rules and regulations which would stifle the beauty of movement which he displays so very well? Yet there are those who would.

As mentioned in the chapter on action, some would have rules made that would certainly have a disasterous effect on the performance Morgan, and possibly cause unfavorable repercussions within the breed. They refuse to see that showing Morgans as show horses will not bring about the ruination of the breed. Present trends indicate that the breeder of show-type Morgans has far from departed from the true Morgan characteristics of conformation. Indeed since conformation and type count about as much as action in show-ring rules for Morgans (40 percent type and conformation, 60 percent performance, except in Championship Stake Classes where it is 50-50) they are naturally considered of prime importance in a breeding program.

Two Camps

Most of the criticism comes from those breeders who seldom if ever show horses themselves and who have always stressed the Morgan's use as a pleasure horse. They are apprehensive, they say, about the loss of the basic aims of producing a horse that can and will do any job equally well, from plowing to trail riding. They fear that the trend toward "show type" will contribute to the loss of the basic Morgan attribute, which is its versatility. Actually, it seems that way of going causes the most fireworks. There are those who absolutely abhor the thought of the weighted shoe and shrink in horror from the sight of a 4- or 4½-inch toe on a Morgan. To see a Morgan in the ring going a wild trot only seems to remind them that more and more the Morgan is being recognized as an outstanding show horse, when they would much prefer to have him racking up honors on the competitive trail rides instead. That Morgans can do both will be shown later in the chapter on the Morgan as a pleasure horse.

So it would seem that Morgan enthusiasts are divided into two camps, each of the firm opinion that his idea of the perfect Morgan is the right one. Each camp has its points, aptly made: but none can deny the fact that the publicity gained for the breed has resulted in its greatest demand since the heyday of the roadster.

Many breeders and owners feel that their Morgans should be equally at home in the show ring and on the trail (many Morgans are filling this requirement to perfection and that is very well and good, if it can be done). The difficulty comes about, however, when these same owners appear at a prominent show (as opposed to the small local show) and, entering their trail/show horse in a Morgan Performance Class, are soundly beaten by Morgans who are used solely for performance classes. They cry, "It isn't fair," and the use of the ill-fitting term "Saddlebred" is mumbled about with varying intensity. The fact that this trail/show horse may have won the Morgan Pleasure Class seldom seems to cool the situation—"it probably should have won the Stake, too!"

Of course this sort of thing goes on at shows regardless of the breed or division—it is part and parcel of showing. Everyone naturally thinks his horse is best or he wouldn't be there in the first place. No show was ever held that didn't have some dissention among its exhibitors. The point being made, though, is that these few dissenters bend the ear of the uninitiated gathered around the stables and ring, causing lots of confusion and giving horse shows a bad name. They harm the breed, too, if they would only stop and consider it. Granted, often a judge can make a mistake in a class of Morgans, if he is unfamiliar with the breed and its show-ring requirements. Many a furious exhibitor has tongue-lashed a judge unmercifully because his horse "never made a mistake" yet the judge ignored it and pinned a showier horse that perhaps didn't take its canter as easily, or pranced instead of walked in the class. If this same person would take into consideration the fact that the judge was looking for a performance horse in the class and wanted a horse with presence, with manners secondary, he might realize that his own horse, while letter-perfect in its manners, might have lacked the brilliance of the one pinned the winner. But just because a Morgan is high-going and decidedly showy, it doesn't make him any less a typical Morgan that the winner of the Pleasure Class is typical. Indeed as far as type is concerned, the best seem to be found in Performance Classes, because type counts more in these classes than in the Pleasure Class.

Versatility the Morgan has *as a breed,* and this fact we loudly proclaim abroad. Occasionally it is found in an individual—one which is an excellent trail horse as well as an outstanding performance horse. Giving credit where it is due, there is first-rate advertising in the little horse that wins the Morgan Pleasure Class, the Open Road Hack *and* the Morgan Saddle Stake—but just how often does this happen? Especially at the big shows?

Realizing that a performance horse (and by this we mean a show Morgan), if ridden daily or even less often on the trail during the show season, is bound to lack the zip and ginger needed for a Performance Class, most folks who have one good enough for show, wouldn't think of "beating him around the trails." It is because too much saddle work will take the edge off a performer and cost him that extra difference in how he presents himself in the ring, that owners of show animals prefer to keep their horses off the trails during the show season. Yet there is usually no reason for keeping a Morgan *just* for show purposes, unless he is the occasional—and rare —individual who isn't a good trail ride anyway. Just as the show Morgan may lack the zip if ridden more than necessary, so does the trail horse often lack the same brilliance in the ring demanded in the Performance Class. He may be collected and balanced but he will be beaten if competing with horses that possess show-ring presence and animation.

A long objective look at the situation and a full realization of what it takes to make an outstanding Morgan show horse would put an end to much of the criticism of the performance horse. Breeding, training and careful handling make a show horse, and if a horse has benefited from this handling and training, it should *not* make him an outcast as a Morgan, provided he possesses the necessary characteristics of type and conformation.

Increasing the Classes

One answer to the problem might be an increase in the support of the shows which offer a full division of Morgan classes, thereby assuring classes of all types for Morgans at the shows. There are many owners who, while grumbling about the way things are going in the show ring, never make any effort themselves to get out and show their own horses. If they would support them, it is a certainty that many shows would offer more classes so that pleasure Morgans would not be required to compete on equal terms with performance Morgans. If half the energy exerted on complaints and grumbling was devoted to convincing show committees that a full Morgan division would be an asset to their show, many of the conflicts would end with increased activities for *all* exhibitors at the shows. If all the complainers got behind the breed and exhibited regularly, thus providing a show of strength, as it were, there would be a tremendous surge of enthusiasm from show committees—who are always apprehensive about offering classes that might fail to fill. The success of showing horses of any breed depends as much on the backers of the respective breed as it does on the committee that runs the show. If they can be guaranteed an abundance of entries in a division, most shows will go to extremes to include any classes which the exhibitors might request. But just as quickly will they drop a division that is weak in its support. There is always another to take its place.

CHAMPIONS AND TYPES

Of all the top performance Morgans that have been in the limelight in recent years, it can be said that none of them really lacked Morgan type. It is true that there was some variation in height (as there has been down through the years), but in conformation and type

Budd

WINDCREST DONA LEE, *Miss Pat Kelley up, showing championship form.*

they have all been far-above-average individuals, with a consistent uniformity.

The bloodlines of these winners have been varied, and no one family can be said to have dominated the winners' circles completely. Government farm breeding has been represented by such famous names as Ulendon, Orland Leader, Black Sambo, Orland Vigildon, Riviera and Madalin. The Upwey breeding, with its outcross to Saddleblood, produced the champion Upwey Ben Don, his great daughter Windcrest Dona Lee, Upwey Ebony Princess, Windcrest Donfield and the speedy Saracen. Sealect blood, coming down from Ethan Allen 3rd, produced Cornwallis, Parade and Sealect of Windcrest. Lippitt breeding, based almost exclusively on old-type Morgans, is represented by Lippitt Dusky Kate and Lippitt Duplicate (full sisters), Supersam and Lippitt Mandate. Flyhawk, Senator Graham, Dennis K and Bonfire are representatives of bloodlines of Midwestern origin which have produced outstanding Morgans.

Probably the most outstanding of all contemporary Morgan show horses is the illustrious mare Windcrest Dona Lee owned by Mrs. Antoinette Kelley of Chester, Vermont. This mare, sired by the champion in his own right, Upwey Ben Don, has defeated every Morgan—stallion, mare and gelding—to show against her. With a trot to make any Saddlebred breeder envious, she has excelled in harness as well as under saddle—and has been Grand Champion Model Mare at the National Morgan Horse Show as well. Her sire, Upwey Ben Don, was by Upwey King Benn, himself by Upwey King Peavine, who was a registered American Saddlebred. Her dam was Ingrid, who was by one of the best government-bred stallions, Mansfield. The percentage folk may deplore the Saddleblood outcross which produced Dona Lee, but no one can deny that she is an outstanding mare in every way.

On the old-Morgan-blood side of the show-ring fence, Lippitt Duplicate, a high-percentage mare of excellent pedigree and type, is one example of an outstanding performance horse produced by old Vermont blood. While not shown too extensively, this 15.0-hand mare found great favor in the ring whenever she was exhibited. At the 1954 National she won the Model Mares Four Years Old and Over

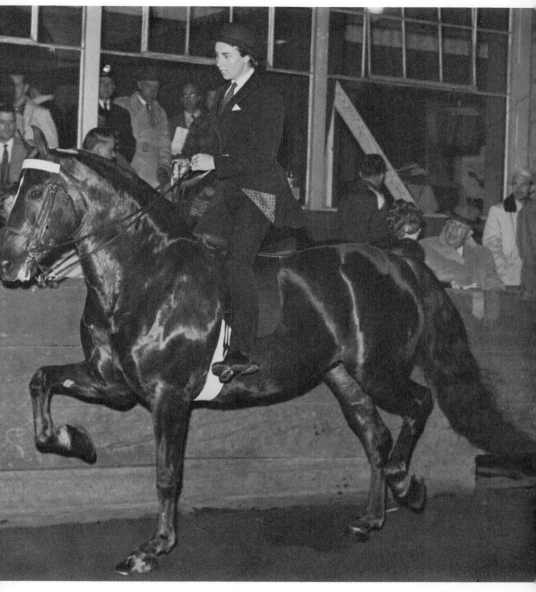

*One of Orcland Leader's well-known daughters, Madalin, the author up,
winning an over-15 hands class.*

from a huge class of more than forty entries. She was equally out-standing under saddle, having a high, brilliant trot that was completely natural to her.

The point to derive from these two examples of bloodlines in Morgans is that greatness can come from any line. So a drop of Saddle-blood doesn't necessarily produce champions—nor is high percentage a sure thing either. Outstanding show horses have come from every line, and careful training only is needed to bring them out.

To conclude this chapter on Morgans in the show ring, it might be interesting to give here a brief description of one of the most hotly contested classes for Morgans in the country: the Championship Saddle Stake at the National Morgan Horse Show. Here you will find the best in the nation battling it out as if their very lives depended upon the outcome. Here the tension, which has been mounting throughout the show, quivers like a taut bowstring. This is the most coveted award of all . . . the highest honor . . . the greatest prize; this is the moment when all the hours of training become manifest. The gate swings open. And at a rousing trot the cream of America's show Morgans flash into the ring, manes and tails streaming, hoofs shaking the ground in rhythmic cadence to the heartbeats of the watchers. The railbirds know the spectacle to come and the grand-stand crowds move forward in their seats in anticipation.

With ears sharp and eyes ashine the Morgans spin along the rail to the cheers of owners, friends, stablehands and onlookers. Even the grandstand folk can feel the tension; the tremendous enthusiasm is as contagious as measles in a kindergarten. Morgan people have a tendency to get exceedingly emotional about their entries, and you can be sure every rider in the ring is riding to win. A now-or-never spirit charges the atmosphere. The horses sense it too, for it is obvious they are swept on by the enthusiasm of their riders. The pounding hoofbeats, the glistening, groomed-to-the-nth-degree coats of the horses, the determined expressions of the riders, the hoots and squeals from the rail as a favorite flashes by, all contribute to the thrilling spectacle. At the completion of the three gaits in each direction, the horses are stripped for conformation—that is, they are judged for type and conformation, which counts 50 percent in all Morgan Championship Stake Classes. Meanwhile shaking hands grip the ring fence. The tension now is at the breaking point. When the ringmaster asks the riders to remount their horses everyone wonders if the judges will call out a few to work again. It usually happens that they do. And then, when the watchers think they can't stand another moment of suspense, the horses are asked to line up. The moment is at hand. The judges confer briefly, glance once more at the class, mark and sign their cards and slowly walk across the ring to the judges' stand. A silence as deep as the grave settles over the crowd. To the riders it seems an eternity till the judges' cards are in the hands of the announcer. Hushed voices are heard along the rail as fingers are fervently crossed. The announcer clears his throat . . . a feeling of power emanates from him. All eyes are on him as he calls out the number of the winner—the Champion!

Like a clap and roar of thunder the crowd finds its voice. A horse moves out of line and trots down the length of the ring to receive his ribbon and trophy. The tricolor glistens as the late afternoon sun glances off the satin streamers, and the silver trophy reflects a blue-ribbon grin. The Grand Champion Saddle Horse of the National Morgan Show arches his neck to receive his ribbon, then poses for photographers, his ears ringing to the din of the ovation around him. The Reserve Champion is pinned with almost equal enthusiasm from the rail. Only when the last ribbon, the eighth, flutters from a bridle does the last degree of tension snap. For in a show of this magnitude any ribbon at all is cause enough for a celebration.

What makes this Saddle Stake the most popular class at this show or any show with a Morgan division? It is the action . . . action and brilliance and showmanship. Without these things, the Morgan just couldn't have come so far as he has in recent years. This cannot be stressed enough. His versatility, no matter how great, alone could never have put him in the position he now occupies in the show ring. It is the beauty of line and beauty of movement that attract, no matter what the critics might say. The Morgan can be and is a show horse—to stifle him in this endeavor is folly.

IX

For Pleasure

JUST exactly what is a pleasure horse? How is it different from, say, a field hunter or a working stock horse or a polo pony? The difference is specialization. The hunter is required to excel at a specific task: to follow and keep up with hounds. The stock horse's job is working cattle, and the polo pony is trained specifically to twist and turn at speed and keep his eye on the ball. Many people who are fond of horses indulge in these special fields and prefer to limit their horse activities to their own sphere of interest. People who have show horses of various breeds, and prefer the excitement and glamor of the show ring to the sound of the hounds and the crack of a polo mallet, confine their interest to the call of the show circuits.

But the vast majority of horse owners keep horses for pleasure riding. They find, in the easy companionship of a good horse on the trail, more downright enjoyment in just following a path in the woods than they would in sailing over walls at a mad gallop or trying to outrace a competitor for a white wooden ball.

The pleasure horse has become increasingly popular in the years since World War II, with a growing number of people becoming interested in horses and riding. More and more adults are finding that the relaxation and healthful exercise which go along with owning a horse have benefited them greatly in the frantic rush of the times. A good horse is a companion that does not make unreasonable demands; nor does he back-talk you when all you wish for is peace and

Mr. and Mrs. J. Cecil Ferguson on their matched mares.

quiet, and he will greet you with a friendly nicker when you come to the stable. Even the tending of him, if you truly like horses, becomes a ritual rather than a chore. There is a certain satisfaction in carefully grooming your horse and seeing the reward of your efforts in his gleaming coat; or in putting down a fresh, crisp bed of straw in his stall and watching him roll luxuriously in its clean, crackling softness. If you like horses, your own stable, no matter how modest, is your pride and your retreat from the hustle and bustle of everyday living. To saddle up and head for the hills is the best prescription ever written for jangled nerves and frayed tempers. A good pleasure

horse can make you forget you had words with the boss or that to-
morrow a big conference is waiting with its attendant headaches. All
the worries and frustrations seem to fall away with the gentle clop,
clop of your horse's hoofs on the soft ground. Many are the people
who never thought to own a horse who have found and are finding
horse ownership a most rewarding experience.

There are at least two prime requisites necessary to the ideal pleasure horse: he must have a pleasant manner and a good disposition,
and he should have easy gaits that are comfortable to his rider. His
nature should be companionable and he should show interest in his
surroundings and the events taking place in them. In other words, it
is just no fun riding a machine. A horse may be beautifully broken
and trained and still lack the best attributes of the *ideal* pleasure
horse.

The pleasure horse should in a sense be a pet, and yet not spoiled.
He should be a responsive and intelligent companion but not the
master. Nothing is worse than an animal made willful and unruly by
an overindulgent owner. Little is more unpleasant than riding a
horse that has got away with murder and fights you at every turn
because he has been allowed to have his own way before. He should
be on his mettle, yet agreeable to his rider's whims.

The Morgan has proved himself in countless ways to be the ideal
pleasure horse for young and old. His natural docility, coupled with
a personality that almost defies adequate description, makes him the
favorite of owners everywhere. His hardiness and easy-keeping qualities, his endurance and versatility make the Morgan in demand the
country over.

Regardless of whether you prefer Western tack and style of riding
or English, the Morgan is equally at home. And indeed many owners
ride them both ways depending on whatever whim seizes them. Morgans give a good appearance either way, with smooth gaits that lend
themselves to any task.

The little bay mare who was my first horse stood only a slight 14.2,
and yet her versatility and temperament amazed all who knew her.
At the age of three years she had negotiated every jumpable stone
wall within a radius of twenty miles of her stable. She hauled us all

". . . equal to any task and eager to go along."

over the back roads in a heavy cart for hours at a time and whether she was tacked up in a stock saddle or a Pariani (forward-seat jumping saddle) or ridden bareback, it made little difference in her outlook. Long hours on the trail with frequent all-out gallops, racing against friends' hunters, or a myriad of walls and logs to jump *en route* never seemed to wear her out. She would always come home with a spring in her walk and ears cocked eagerly for the familiar road. She won her share of ribbons at the shows and taught innumerable children to ride. She experienced parades and picnics and even the Grand March in a Rodeo. She took us swimming in the Sound, and in a work harness raked hay with a creaking old horse rake swaying behind her. At the age of *nineteen* she won blues at the shows, amazing people by her youthful appearance and action. Her legs were free of any blemishes all her life and never was she lame despite her varied tasks. This little mare was a pleasure horse in every sense of the word. She was companion and friend and confidante. She was a member of the family, a pet who would eat ice cream and apple pie; was a means of transportation when the car was gone, and was the heroine of the neighborhood kids. At times she could be a spoiled brat but an occasional display of independence never damaged her reputation, for everyone liked and admired her too much to remember it.

JUST PLAIN FUN

This is the way Morgan pleasure horses should be: equal to any task and willing and eager to go along with their riders' whims. No assignment should be too difficult for a Morgan at least to try.

A great many people who own pleasure Morgans find an occasional horse show a cheery diversion and a chance for social contact with other horse owners. They enter their Morgans in open classes as well as Morgan classes and often come away with ribbons won against stiff competition from other breeds. This can be exceedingly gratifying if you have raised and trained your own horse.

I remember the show circuit I used to make with my little mare in New Hampshire. Almost every Sunday in the summer there would be a local show somewhere within the White Mountain district, and

off we would go. These shows were what I have always referred to as "fun shows." There was little at stake and everyone attended for the good time that was certain to be had. The horses shown were good (but maybe not Madison Square Garden material) and the competition stimulating. The arrangement for entry fees was original and conducive to filling classes: one flat sum was paid and the exhibitor could take his horse in any or all classes! It can be seen easily that this sort of arrangement could be made-to-order for Morgan owners, as everything from Bridle Path Hack to Western Stock Horse could be entered if one had a versatile horse. It was possible to win a goodly number of ribbons as well as proving your horse's ability and versatility.

However the fun of the White Mountain shows was not entirely based on ribbon winning, although all enjoyed winning, but on the sporting spirit of the participants and the friendly atmosphere that prevailed. Everyone brought not only his horse to the show but his enthusiasm for the sport, and also traveled with his good-natured wit and a wonderful capacity for sociability.

The Easy-to-Please Breed

Not only a pleasing manner and an easy gait make Morgans the ideal pleasure and family horse. For most folks who keep their horses at home and do their own stable work, the added factor of their Morgan's easy-keeping qualities is a strong point in his favor. Morgans require the minimum of feed and usually remain butter-ball fat on it. They thrive on roughing it in the winter—although they do prefer human companionship to being alone.

A Morgan can be hooked to the sleigh one day and have a Western saddle slung over its back the next, and do a sizable number of miles either way without fatigue. When conditioned properly for the task, the Morgans prove their ability and stamina in all types of competitive and non-competitive trail rides over all types of terrain. They are sure-footed and reliable and usually up to any difficulty they may encounter.

The Accommodating Breed

Morgans are America's ideal pleasure horse for young folks and

The Seabrook Four-in-Hand.

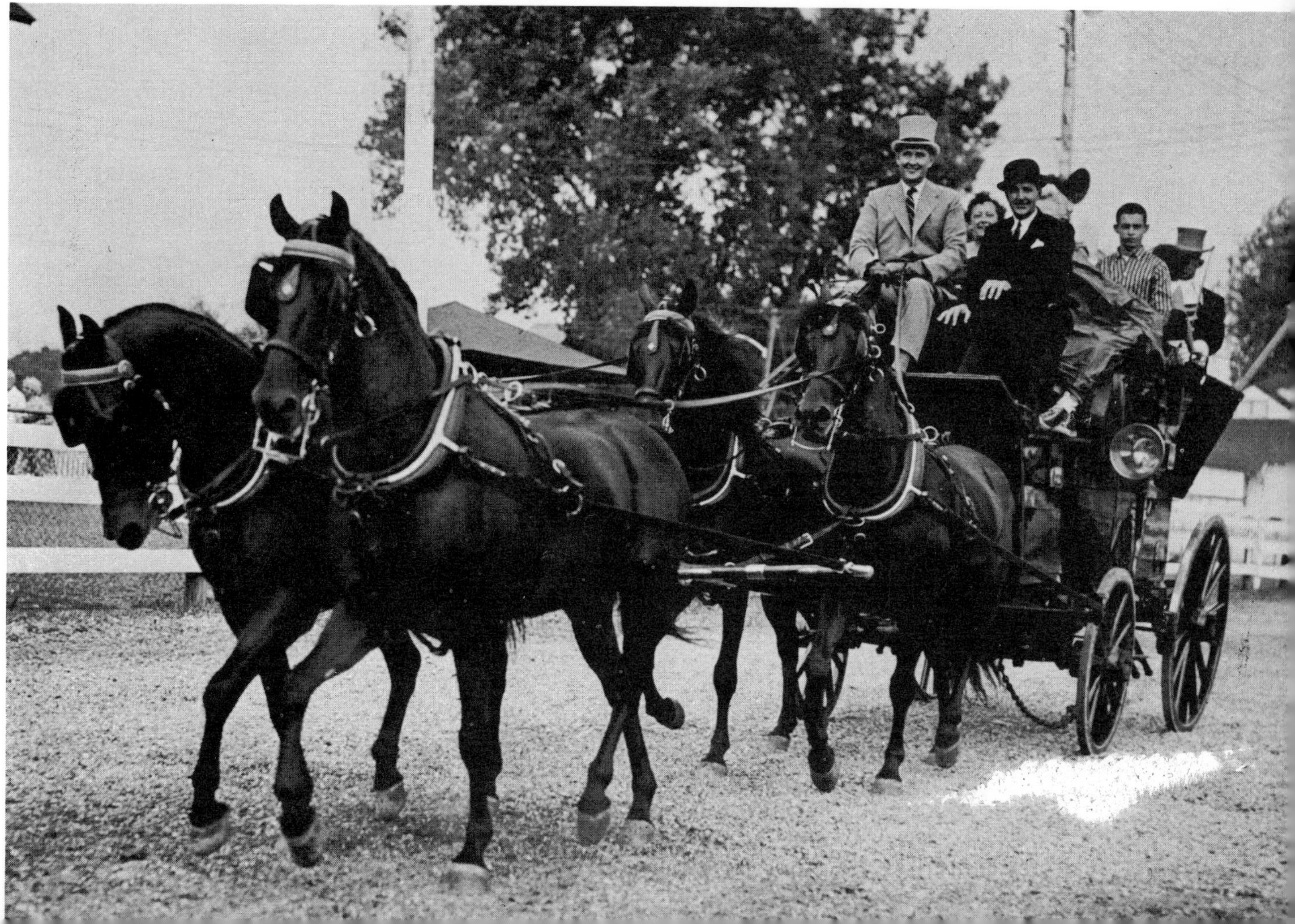

adults, many say, because they are so easily trained. Quick to learn, they usually require fewer lessons than most horses and their intelligence often amazes even their owners.

They almost seem to know what is expected of them before it is asked. The young owners, quick to recognize Morgan versatility, soon have their pride and joy doing everything from speeding down a dirt road at a roadster gait with a pack of cohorts lending keen competition, to cutting the neighbor's Black Angus in the stock-horse manner. Morgan versatility, exploited by the young enthusiast, can reach amazing proportions in some individuals, depending upon the inventiveness of the owners. While the adult owner may have more decorum and prefer to enjoy his Morgan on quiet rides through a dewy meadow at dawn, the kids soon find a most agreeable accomplice in their Morgan when pursuing off-beat horse activities.

THE TRAIL RIDES

It might be interesting here to give some information about the famous 100-Mile Trail Ride which is held annually in the "Morgan country" around Woodstock, Vermont.

A successor to the old 300-Mile Endurance Rides held in Vermont by the cavalry (Vermont was chosen because it offered the best riding country and afforded the most variety in terrain), the 100-Mile Trail Ride was first held in 1936. It was sponsored by The Green Mountain Horse Association and is the oldest competitive trail ride of its type in the United States.

Although only eleven entries turned out for the first ride, each year the event attracted more and more horsemen to the Woodstock area in the late summer. From all parts of the country they came with a mixed variety of horses in tow. The increasing interest brought so many entries that soon a limit had to be placed on the number allowed to compete in the ride. A 50-Mile Pleasure Ride was inaugurated to give more people a chance for group trail riding in the Vermont countryside. Non-competitive, this ride offers a less grueling, equally enjoyable experience on the lovely Vermont trails.

In the 100-mile ride, forty miles must be covered each of the first

two days. Seven hours are allowed for the forty-mile distance, with penalties given for extra time used. On the third day the riders are allowed three hours to complete twenty miles. And all these miles are over rough, tortuous trails that test to the fullest a horse's condition and endurance. Needless to say, the riders must be made of the same stuff as their horses, for the long hours in the saddle can take their toll with the improperly prepared human or equine. Yet it is interesting to note that despite the arduous experience the 100-mile ride affords, the waiting list of those who wish to enter the ride grows each year.

Judges and official veterinarians follow the riders each day and no one escapes their careful scrutiny. Each horse is checked for condition throughout the ride and the judges make their scorings. A rider must time himself carefully during the periods on the trail because no extra time is allowed for unscheduled stops.

The official timer checks every horse as it returns to the stable and records the exact time on each entry. For every three minutes over the time limit, a penalty is imposed. No boots, pads or bandages are allowed on the horses, and equally taboo are liniments or other medications. A horse *must* be in top condition: any sign of soreness leads to disqualification.

What purpose does the 100-Mile Trail Ride serve? you may ask. The answers are many and varied, but the most important reasons are that it increases interest in trail riding and provides a model for other rides, it is a stimulus for developing the endurance of horse and rider, it proves the rewarding knowledge that selection, conditioning and proper care of horses pay off in added enjoyment, and it puts sportsmanship and horsemanship above the glory of winning honors. Riders participate for various reasons, too—for the zest of competition, the camaraderie of kindred spirits and a pure love of horses and riding.

Morgans have always done well in the 100-mile ride since its inception. Over large fields with their representative breeds of light horses, they have won much acclaim and racked up phenominal records. In recent years the records have stood as follows:

1951   *Lightweight Division* (carrying 155-179 pounds): won by TARIK'S GOLDEN LASS, a Morgan mare

1952   *Lightweight Division:* won by MAX, a Morgan gelding; *Sweepstakes:* won by MAX, a Morgan gelding

1953   *Lightweight Division:* won by SONELDON, a Morgan gelding

1954   *Junior Division:* won by QUORUM, a Morgan gelding; *Lightweight Division:* won by SONELDON, a Morgan gelding

1954   *Heavyweight* (carrying 180 or more pounds): won by ARKOMIA, a Morgan mare; *Sweepstakes:* won by ARKOMIA, a Morgan mare

1955   *Sweepstakes:* won by QUORUM, a Morgan gelding

1956   *Junior:* won by DOES, a Morgan gelding

1957   *Lightweight:* won by DOES, a Morgan gelding

1958   *Lightweight:* won by CAPPY SMITH, a Morgan gelding

1959   *Lightweight:* 2nd, TOWNSHEND LADY O' PEACE, a Morgan mare; *Junior:* won by PRINCESS DONNA, a Morgan mare

1960   *Lightweight:* won by TOWNSHEND LADY O' PEACE, a Morgan mare; *Sweepstakes:* won by TOWNSHEND LADY O' PEACE; *Junior:* won by MERRYVALE, a Morgan mare

Because it is such an achievement merely to finish the arduous course, all who complete the entire ride receive ribbons and certificates.

In trail rides all over the country Morgans take the limelight wherever they appear. Their beauty and lively interest as well as their enduring qualities make them outstanding in any group of light horses.

LET HORSES ENJOY IT TOO

Considering that the versatility of a horse is mostly a matter of his disposition and training, Morgan owners endeavor to develop the many diversified talents found in the breed. They boast of the fact that their horses are equally at home in any tack and in harness and yet still, when collected, have enough action and presence to perform in the show ring. But as mentioned earlier in the chapter on showing Morgans, many owners can go too far and expect too much.

I have always been of the firm opinion that modern Morgans must be divided into separate classes. Although their conformation should be similar, it is to be expected that their temperaments will differ. The demands of today's show-ring competition have altered the situation so that performance Morgans must be outstanding as such, and equally the pleasure Morgan must be well qualified in *his* class. I maintain that a Morgan with naturally quiet disposition should not be shaken up to make him labor in vain while competing with a Morgan with obvious show ability. It is far better to take that born pleasure horse and develop him into the best all-round pleasure horse possible. Take him into competition with other breeds on equal footing and prove the Morgan's superiority! Train him to do well anything that might be asked of him, whether it be jumping a wall or holding a rope in a stock-horse class. Condition him properly and take him in the 100-mile ride. Enjoy him on the trail, riding with friends. Cultivate all you can his fine disposition and easy manner.

What is the point of beating your head against a wall by sending an obviously unqualified pleasure type to a professional trainer with the instructions, and yes, the demand, that he make a show horse of him? It just can't be done successfully and I have seen many a nice Morgan spoiled by just such a move by its owner. Often the horse returns nervous and high-strung where before he was quiet and easy-going. His feet show the evidence of excessively heavy shoeing and his mouth is often damaged by over-bitting and heavy hands. My question has always been: is it really worth it? Would not the money thrown away on trying to make a show horse of the pleasure mount, have been better spent toward purchasing a Morgan of show caliber in the first place? Money notwithstanding, we won't mention what is taken out of the horse in such an arrangement.

Unfortunately some Morgans fall in between the two categories: that is, they have not quite enough ability to compete in the performance class and yet are a bit too hot for the ideal pleasure horse. These individuals can become a real problem to their owners. Some-

Rx for fun: Morgans and youngsters.

times hard work and enough of it will simmer 'em down, but often this type of disposition can't be worn down enough to be considered ideal from a pleasure angle. If you have ever taken a horse on a trail ride—long or short—who did nothing but jig all the way, you will know what is meant by "to hot for a pleasure horse." There is nothing more exasperating than a horse that will not do a flat-footed walk on the trail, and there is nothing more difficult to cure.

A problem noted in this day and age of generally limited bridle trails is the lack of sufficient exercise for the pleasure horse. Often high spirits in evidence in the otherwise quiet animal is nothing more than the result of insufficient work and abundant feed. A well-fed Morgan that hasn't been out in a day or two is expected to have a few humps in his spine, and may need a few miles to get the kinks out before he will settle down. Most owners rather expect this and are prepared for it, but it is enervating to the novice.

If possible, turning a horse out in a paddock or barnyard every day he isn't used will tend to keep the foolishness to a minimum when he is ridden later. Many owners take their horses out and lunge them a few minutes before mounting. Most horses settle down fine after they've uncorked a few good ones, and give no further trouble. High spirits are rather a characteristic of Morgans and indeed of almost any horse kept in good condition, especially in the wintertime. Experienced horsemen realize this, ride out the storm and forget about it. There is no point in making a production over it, for some Morgans just love an opportunity to play with their riders to see "who will win today."

To sum up: Morgans are excellent pleasure horses with gaits suitable for either English or Western tack—or both. They have tremendous personality that improves with attention; they will at least try anything that is asked of them, and will give a fair account of themselves at any task. Their disposition, if properly handled, cannot be bettered; and in conformation and beauty they always seem to stand out in a group. They make excellent long-distance trail horses, good working stock horses, and a few have been outstanding as jumpers. They are almost all equally as good in harness as they are under saddle, and thus make wonderful family horses.

SADWIN

Jeanne Mellin

No account of pleasure Morgans would be complete without mention of one of the most outstanding and extraordinary Morgans in recent years. The little chestnut mare Sadwin, owned by the Ela family of Bolton, Massachusetts, was foaled deep in Vermont's Green Mountains in the village of Townshend. Out of the long-distance trail horse Gladwin and by John A. Darling, a high-percentage stallion of old Vermont breeding, Sadwin is perhaps one of the best-known pleasure horses, in Morgan circles, ever foaled. Her record as a trail horse, family horse, equitation horse and all-round pleasure horse has yet to be equaled.

Foaled in 1931, this diminutive (14.2) Morgan mare has walked, trotted and cantered to glory on innumerable competitive trail rides and has given hundreds of children their first horse-borne thrill. She has competed in the 100-Mile Trail Rides since 1937, when she was the winner of the Best Trail Horse award. Her winnings continued every year through 1945. In 1941 she was named Morgan Horse of the Year when she won not only the 100-mile ride but the 80-Mile Maine Trail Ride as well.

In the show ring, too, this little Morgan often led the way. In the days when the National Morgan Horse Show was held in Woodstock it is known that Sadwin was *ridden* to Woodstock from Townshend, Vermont; where, *after* competing in the 100-mile ride, she was shown in the Morgan show (then only in the afternoon) and then she was *ridden home* after the show—the SAME DAY! This alone would make Sadwin remarkable.

But endurance is far from being her only claim to fame. She has been shown in all types of classes at the shows, from Western Pleasure, to Pleasure Driving, to Equitation, and has garnered her share of ribbons all along the way. She has nurtured the first bloom of "horse craziness" in scores of children, and through it all has kept the remarkable even disposition for which the Morgan is famed.

Trustworthy, lovable and enduring has been Sadwin, giving to her owners almost three decades of service and devotion. She is proof that Pleasure Morgans are really a pleasure—a joy—in every sense of the word.

X

For Stock Work
... and War

THE MORGAN is a natural as a stock and Western pleasure
animal, and let no one tell you that *all* cowboys ride Quarter
horses. A great many ride Morgans and wouldn't have it any other
way. Despite all the Quarter-horse propaganda, the demand for
Morgans in the West is increasing yearly. The growing enthusiasm
for the breed is noted by the formation of many new local Morgan
clubs in the Western states, through whose efforts the Morgan cause
is being furthered amidst the ranks of other light breeds striving for
recognition.

Because of a tremendous demand for purebred horses for both
work and pleasure during the past few years, each light breed association or club has stepped up its advertising and promotion program to meet the competition. Having supporters with equal enthusiasm but possibly less capital, the Morgan has been temporarily
eclipsed by other breeds in American horse publications, thereby
being out of the spotlight, so to speak. But this condition is no indication of retreat. The Morgan has never been on firmer footing: his
versatility is his greatest ace in the hole.

As a Western pleasure horse he has the conformation and the gait
and certainly the endurance, but let us consider the prerequisites of

the working stock horse and how the Morgan can and does qualify for this type of work.

AT HOME ON THE RANGE

The first requirements in a stock horse are intelligence and dependability. Without these you will never make a good cow horse of an animal, no matter the breed and bloodlines. Regardless of how well trained he is, a horse must be able to think for himself in a ticklish situation when his rider is occupied with problems of his own. The horse must concentrate on the job at hand and keep cool-headed in the bargain. His rider depends on his horse's intelligence as well as his ability. He doesn't want a horse that becomes rattled and upset at a crucial moment, and he expects the animal to do its work on its own and not require cues from the rider at every step. When a horse displays this sort of sixth sense when working cattle he is said to have "cow-savvy." And you can be sure that without this cow-savvy you do not have a cow horse—no matter how much he may look the part. A good stock horse must be able to outthink and out-maneuver the cow in his work. Consequently the agility and surefootedness that come with natural ability and careful training cannot be overestimated.

Conformation, too, is of prime importance in the working stock horse. Experience has proved that the compactly built, blocky horse has a definite advantage over the rangy, long-legged animal with a

Big Bill B

JOHN GEDDES—*champion working stock horse.*

lot of daylight under him. For the twisting and turning, the iron stamina and surefootedness that are demanded of the stock horse, a ranginess in conformation is a definite handicap. Not only will the smaller, blocky horse carry weight better but he is usually much more agile doing it.

It is argued by many that the ideal stock horse, the animal most suited to this type of work, is the much-vaunted Quarter horse. He is the one seen most often in the rodeo arena and admittedly has a terrific burst of speed useful in competitive events. He is certainly popular for ranch work and any job requiring Western tack. But who's to deny that the Morgan, if as carefully trained, cannot hold his own with the Quarter horse, especially in the area of work-a-day ranch chores? His conformation, temperament and intelligence, his quick, energetic way of going and his easy gaits and endurance make him a natural for every facet of ranch work. It is one of the Morgan's great stocks in trade that he can do yeoman duty on the range and trail and still have the beauty and action for parade or show.

A Morgan has, and always has had, style to go along with his varied abilities. From little hard-working Justin Morgan down to the present day there has been somewhat of a show-off tendency in the Morgan's personality. So all that is needed to set it in motion is a few people with admiring glances standing around. Morgans, in the vernacular of the theater, are just hams at heart. Their versatility has been exploited, but their downright good looks and perky attentiveness shouldn't be taken lightly. In this day and age horsemen want a mount that not only can do the type of work meted out to it but one that will stand out in a group by its appearance. Here the Morgan has no rival. He looks the part of the stock horse; his conformation is right, and if properly trained he can cut out a steer and hold a rope with any breed going and still have the edge on them all for beauty.

The Morgan popularity as a working stock horse has fallen behind the Quarter horse mainly from lack of breed promotion, not lack of natural ability. It is the fashion nowadays to ride a Quarter horse, and that breed association has pushed this thesis to the utmost. Yet the Morgan, as versatile as he is, could perhaps outstrip the Quarter

ADMIRAL

horse were he given the necessary shot in the arm of extensive advertising and nationwide promotion. His qualifications as an *all-round* Western horse far outrival any other breed; a fact that is steadily arousing much interest in the stronghold of the Quarter horse.

It is, however, in the field of pleasure riding that the Morgan can really snatch the crown, for here beauty counts to a marked degree. The Morgan with his flowing mane and tail and his high-headed alert countenence has them all taking a back seat! Just ride a bright-eyed, sprightly Morgan in any group of pleasure horses and see the reaction on the sidelines. And when you return from the ride on the same quick-stepping steed you'll have chalked up another sizable score for the Morgan horse.

Consider the case of Aunt Suzie coming to visit and declining the invitation to "ride Western" because she prefers her jodhpurs to levis. When you own a Morgan you merely remove the stock saddle, replace it with Auntie's "postage stamp" and watch the smooth conversion. Or if Aunt Suzie brings the kids, hitch that Morgan to the express wagon and take 'em all for a ride. You can be back working stock or riding fence on Monday morning with the same horse, and one none the worse for the break in routine.

Stock-horse type and Morgan type are essentially similar. As can be seen in earlier illustrations, points of conformation of the typy Morgan fit the requirements for the stock horse equally well. The good feet and legs which are so necessary to a working horse are found in the Morgan, and although the hindquarters and forearms and gaskins may not appear as heavily muscled as in the Quarter horse, they are equally strong and powerful. The close-coupling and short back are Morgan characteristics; and his medium length of neck and intelligent head and expression complete the picture of ideal stock horse type.

OUTSTANDING EARLY BREEDERS

Proof of the Morgan's excellence as a stock horse has been found by the number of Western breeders of Morgans for this purpose. As early as the 1880s Richard Sellman, a native of Maryland, established his Mountain Vale Ranch in Texas and around the turn of the century was known to have owned forty thousand acres of good Texas land, eight thousand sheep, four thousand registered Black Angus cattle and four hundred head of registered Morgan horses. He was at that time the largest breeder of registered Morgans in the country: it is said that on many occasions he was able to ship Morgan mares by the carload and include a suitable stallion to head the herd!

The Sellman Studs

Mr. Sellman's objective was to produce true Morgan type, for he was very much opposed to the heavy outcrossing to the Standardbred blood in those early days. He set out to prove that the original Morgan type could be preserved, purchasing the best representatives of this type he could find in the North and East and shipping them to his Texas ranch for breeding purposes. The fine stallion RED OAK, a full brother to BENNINGTON, was purchased from the government farm. Five other excellent stallions—MAJOR GORDON 4924, GOLD MEDAL 4840, GOLDEN 5691, GOLDEN ROD 6674 and MAJOR ANTOINE 4776—were included in the breeding program. His top stud, however, was ADMIRAL 4871. Sired by the renowned show-ring star Jubilee De Jarnette (by Jubilee Lambert, by Daniel Lambert and out of Lady de Jarnette), this handsome chestnut stallion got some of the most outstanding Morgans of the day. RED BIRD, one of his best sons, headed the stud at the Swenson Brothers' SMS Ranch.

Morgans were Dick Sellman's consuming passion, and being financially able to indulge himself in the raising of them he had acquired the best, both in stallions and mares. HEADLIGHT MORGAN 4863, by ETHAN ALLEN 2ND 406, dam by Hale's Green Mountain, by Gifford, was considered at the time (1911) to be the nearest to the original Justin Morgan and was awarded a silver cup by The Morgan Horse Club for his excellence. He was the exact type Mr. Sellman wished to preserve on his Texas ranch. Consequently, this famous stallion which had made such a name for himself in New England was purchased by Sellman and taken to the Mountain Vale Ranch. The

horse was at the time twenty-one years old but, as with many old Morgan studs, he hardly appeared his age. The choicest mares and fillies of the ranch were selected to be bred to this fine stallion. The following spring a foal crop which in every way met expectations appeared to prove old Headlight's great worth as a sire. Unfortunately, however, Dick Sellman's pleasure in his horses was to be short-lived after the first crop of Headlight's foals arrived; his health began failing fast and death soon after separated him from his beloved Morgans. A short time later his Mountain Vale Ranch was broken up and his good Morgans scattered throughout the West. California absorbed the majority of them to become, at the time, the state producing the largest number of Morgans in the country, outranking even Vermont. Old Headlight Morgan is said to have lived to be thirty-two years of age.

The Swensons

The SMS Ranch in Stamford, Texas, mentioned above, was established in 1883 by the Swenson Brothers for the purpose of raising

U C MENTION, *fresh from a victory in an English Pleasure Stake, returns to win a Western Pleasure Stake.*

Tarrance

outstanding cow horses. The foundation stock was a Spanish-Arabian cross and experiments were made with Thoroughbred-Standardbred, Saddlebred, grade Clydesdales and grade Percherons, giving adequate (and sometimes not so adequate) results, but not exactly the type of horse desired. In 1914 two Morgan stallions, GOTCH and Red Bird (by Dick Sellman's Admiral), were acquired along with some of the Sellman mares. The SMS Ranch then began producing both registered and grade Morgans for a number of years for use as stock horses. Later the Morgan blood was crossed with Arabian, and outstanding cutting horses were produced from this breeding.

Roland Hill

Probably the most famous of Western breeders of Morgan horses was the late Roland G. Hill of Tres Pinos, California. Mr. Hill, a show judge and breeder, was the owner of the Horse-Shoe Cattle Company, a huge sprawling ranch covering vast areas of California and neighboring Nevada. Few among Morgan breeders on the west coast have not been acquainted with the work and the horses of Roland Hill. No other single person has been so responsible for the popularity of the Morgan horse in California. His use of Morgans as stock horses on his ranch was valid proof that the breed was extremely qualified for this type of work. Great numbers of them were raised for cow horses and breeding stock, and subsequently Mr. Hill became California's largest and best-known breeder of purebred Morgans.

Mr. Hill acquired his first Morgans when he purchased a band of twenty-five mares at the Sellman Ranch dispersal in 1923 and it wasn't long before he was in the Morgan business in a big way. Then, when he went East and purchased the young stallion QUERIDO —a full brother to MANSFIELD—he assured the success of the Morgan venture, for this good son of Bennington-Artemisia sired some of the finest cow-savvyin' Morgans Californians had ever seen. Colts by Querido were soon found to possess disposition and substance and breeders throughout the West soon were beating a path to the door to get hold of the Querido stock. Broodmares of exceptional quality sired by Querido gained the stallion much recognition in the West.

Later, when faced with the problem of a stud to use on Querido's daughters, Mr. Hill spent a number of fruitless years of searching before again returning East to find a certain type of stallion suitable for his operation. It wasn't until he saw SONFIELD, a son of Mansfield and Quietude, that he was satisfied that he had at last found the horse he had sought so long. The choice of Sonfield proved to be a wise one, for the cross produced the desired results. The Querido-Sonfield bloodlines produced fine working stock horses, Western pleasure horses and far-above-average breeding stock.

In *The Western Horseman* of September 1949 J. M. Lawrence had an article dealing with the Morgan horse in which he stated:

"In a high percentage of cases the type, conformation and performance of these horses [Querido-Sonfield line] is entirely satisfactory. In halter and performance classes, and in open competition in the shows throughout the state [California] the horses carrying these bloodlines many times have held the championship spot. At the California State Horseman's Convention show in Santa Rosa, October, 1948, a son of Sonfield, out of a Querido mare, was Grand Champion Morgan; a granddaughter of Sonfield was reserve Grand Champion. Year after year, the get of Sonfield win. These shows are, of course, open to Morgans of any family and are judged by men from all parts of the country. The winnings, then, of this line of breeding can only be attributed to their excellence. . . ."

On many occasions, Mr. Hill himself stated that "Mansfield and his line were the best-producing family in the breed." Certainly with his wide range of experience and successful production of high-class Morgan stock horses, Mr. Hill proved his theory to be correct.

There are a great many present-day breeders of Morgans in the West who confidently feel that the breed has a bright future as a Western pleasure horse and working stock horse despite the rise of the Quarter horse and the so-called color breeds (Appaloosa, Palomino and Pinto). Throughout the area west of the Mississippi the Morgan has gained increasingly greater recognition in the last few years. Much has been accomplished by the local breed organizations through sponsoring all-Morgan shows and Morgan classes at established shows. With these enthusiastic folk behind it, the Morgan should not be taking a back seat to any breed of light horse in the future.

IN THE CIVIL WAR

The same qualities that make the Morgan an ideal working stock horse on Western ranches—his intelligence, maneuverability and stamina—were also at a premium in the cavalry horse. It is impos-

HORSES
Wanted!

DURA WARREN will be at the

HOTEL, IN ROYALTON,

On Wednesday, Nov. 27th, 1861,

and wishes to buy several good, sound, and kind Horses for

CAVALRY USE.

Must stand fifteen hands high and weigh about one thousand pounds. Any one having such a Horse or Horses to sell will meet him at the above place.

Royalton, November 19th, 1861.

sible to determine how much the performance of Morgans in battle during the War Between the States was responsible for their introduction later as stock horses. Be this as it may, and notwithstanding the field marshals who have been immortalized on improbable white chargers, it can be said that the Morgan made notable contributions as a breed during the Civil War.

The First Vermont

Specifically, the 1st Vermont Regiment was mounted exclusively on Morgans, one thousand of them from the northern hills of the state. And they were reported to be the best cavalry mounts and artillery horses in the entire Union Army. The First Vermont was the first cavalry unit to take the field from the New England states in 1861. One daily newspaper, the Newark (New Jersey) *Advertizer* described the march of the First Vermont cavalry through the city this way:

"The Green Mountain boys arrived about four o'clock and marched up Market Street amid the liveliest tokens of enthusiasm. . . . The horses are small, compact and sinewy and evidently capable of great endurance. It was the general remark that so splendid a body of animals had never been seen together in this city."

That the regiment lived up to its appearance is history, for nothing but the highest praise was accorded the men from Vermont and the brave little horses they rode. In seventy-five major battles and skirmishes, some of the bloodiest of the war, the First Vermont displayed the stalwart courage which was so much a part of its heritage. Of the original one thousand Morgans which answered the call to the colors, two hundred survived to the end of the war; records state that some of these were brought back to their native Vermont.

—and Winchester

Probably one of the most famous single events of the war was accomplished by General Philip Sheridan on October 19, 1864, when he galloped down from Winchester, Virginia, to Cedar Creek to rally his scattered troops after a fierce Confederate attack. Sheridan's mount that fateful day was a Morgan: a coal-black gelding he called RIENZI. The horse, of the Black Hawk line, was large by Morgan standards, being 16 hands high and powerfully built. He was greatly

RIENZI *from a photograph taken nearly a century ago.*

admired for his strength and tremendous endurance. Given to Sheridan by Captain A. P. Campbell of the 2nd Michigan Cavalry, Rienzi was ridden by the general on some of the war's most arduous campaigns, and although the horse was wounded on several occasions, he miraculously escaped death under fire.

He was the participant in many a forced march and pushed from sunup until sundown with scant rations at the day's end, yet he never showed signs of the exhaustion which might have been expected. Sheridan in his memoirs wrote of the horse: "From that time [when he was given the horse by Campbell] till the close of the war I rode him almost continuously, in every campaign and battle in which I took part, without once finding him overcome by fatigue though on many occasions his strength was severely tested."

On the day of Sheridan's historic ride from Winchester, the Union Army, under heavy fire from the Confederates at Cedar Creek and with ranks split and demoralized, was in retreat. It was the appearance of their general on the mighty black Rienzi that heartened the troops all along the road from Winchester. Cheered on by the general's confidence and encouragement, the troops rallied and restored their broken ranks. As a result of this famous ride the day was saved for the North.

Thomas Buchanan Read, a poet of the time, best captured the spirit of Sheridan's ride in these ringing words:

> Up from the South at break of day,
> Bringing to Winchester fresh dismay,
> The affrighted air with a shudder bore,
> Like a herald in haste to the chieftain's door,
> The terrible grumble, and rumble, and roar,
> Telling the battle was on once more,
> And Sheridan twenty miles away.
>
> And wider still those billows of war,
> Thundered along the horizon's bar;
> And louder yet into Winchester rolled
> The roar of that red sea uncontrolled,
> Making the blood of the listener cold,

As he thought of the stake in that fiery fray,
And Sheridan twenty miles away.

But there is a road from Winchester town,
A good, broad highway leading down;
And there, through the flush of the morning light,
A steed as black as the steeds of night,
Was seen to pass, as with eagle flight,
As if he knew the terrible need;
He stretched away with his utmost speed;
Hills rose and fell; but his heart was gay,
With Sheridan fifteen miles away.

Still sprung from those swift hoofs, thundering south,
The dust, like smoke from the cannon's mouth;
Or the trail of a comet, sweeping faster and faster,
Foreboding to traitors the doom of disaster.
The heart of the steed and the heart of the master
Were beating like pris'ners assaulting their walls,
Impatient to be where the battle calls;
Every nerve of the charger was strained to full play,
With Sheridan only ten miles away.

Under his spurning feet, the road
Like an arrowy Alpine river flowed,
And the landscape sped away behind
Like an ocean flying before the wind,
And the steed, like a bark fed with furnace ire,
Swept on, with his wild eye full of fire.
But lo, he is nearing his heart's desire;
He is snuffing the smoke of the roaring fray,
With Sheridan only five miles away.

The first that the General saw were the groups
Of stragglers, and then the retreating troops;
What was done? what to do? a glance told him both.
Then striking his spurs, with a terrible oath,
He dashed down the line, 'mid a storm of huzzahs,

And the wave of retreat checked its course there because
The sight of the master compelled it to pause.
With foam and with dust the black charger was gray;
By the flash of his eye, and the red nostril's play,
He seemed to the whole great army to say:
"I have brought you, Sheridan, all the way
From Winchester, down to save the day."

Hurrah! hurrah for Sheridan!
Hurrah! hurrah for horse and man!
And when their statues are placed on high
Under the dome of the Union sky,
The American soldiers' Temple of Fame,
There with the glorious General's name
Be it said in letters both bold and bright,
"Here is the steed that saved the day
By carrying Sheridan into the fight,
From Winchester—twenty miles away!"

Morgans were used in the Indian Wars as cavalry mounts and even in World War I they saw service across the Atlantic. The old Morgan hardiness and endurance never went unnoticed wherever it was found and made a lasting impression on horsemen everywhere.

XI

The Club

and The Register

COLONEL Joseph Battell, a native of Middebury, Vermont, had a tremendous admiration and affection for the Morgan horse all his life through. That this affinity for the breed was far from passive is evinced by the herculean amount of effort and seemingly endless research he put forth in compiling a Morgan history and *Register*. This was accomplished with the publication of *The Morgan Horse and Register*, Volume I, which he had privately printed in 1894.

Early in life Colonel Battell began to accumulate as much published information on the Morgan breed as could be found. His correspondence pertaining to the Morgan reached tremendous proportions; letters from hither and yon arrived at Middlebury to cast just a little more light on the subject. Anxiously he awaited the answers to his many queries, hoping as each one arrived that its contents would help untangle some of the early history of the Morgan. He wrote to men who had known some of the old horses and had actually witnessed their activities. He searched out musty records for any fragment of fact to further his cause. Remote pedigrees were ferreted out by him and his assistants, and no stone was left unturned that might shed some glimmer of light on his subject.

Probably his best source of information, and the foundation for the Morgan *Register*, was the excellent *Morgan Horses* by D. C. Linsley of Middlebury, Vermont. Written as an "essay" for a competition sponsored by the Vermont State Agricultural Society, Linsley's book received the award for the First Premium in 1856. The work gave a graphic description of the Morgan family, its history to that time (1856) and pedigrees of about two hundred forty stallions of the breed. The committee making the award to Linsley for his book declared at the time the award was made:

"In consequence of the peculiar merits of this treatise, the Committee feel authorized to commend it to the particular notice of the Society, as one eminently adapted to the wants of the people of this State and as supplying a desideratum long felt, both in regard to the true history of the Morgan horse and in respect to the best methods of its perpetuation. We believe Mr. Linsley has collected all the facts pertaining to his subject which intelligent research and thorough devotion can furnish; and that he has embodied them in an attractive form and with just discrimination. The information relating to the history of the Breed is important, and, we think, can be found in no work yet published; the style in which it is communicated is clear, spirited, and in perfect keeping with the subject discussed.

"When it is considered that the sources of information in regard to the origin and history of the Morgan horse, now obscure at best, are rapidly diminishing, and that Mr. Linsley has rescued so much, which in a short time would have been beyond the reach of the compiler, it must be admitted he has rendered a valuable service to the farmers of the State, and one which, in the judgment of the Committee, the Society ought not to leave unrecognized."

Considerable portions of Linsley's work are to be found in the first Volume of the Morgan *Register,* so valuable did Colonel Battell consider Linsley's researches. He reinvestigated Linsley's pedigrees and found them to be very accurate, and in his introduction to Volume I he stated that "neither trouble nor expense has been spared to learn all the pertinent facts concerning every pedigree.

"In the preparation of the present work," he continued, "and the inquiries and investigations connected therewith, extending over a period of eight years, we have used in correspondence nearly a hundred thousand letters and have personally visited most of the States in the Union, some of them several times, made repeated excursions into the Provinces of Quebec and Ontario and also visited Mexico."

Another source of Morgan pedigrees which Colonel Battell used extensively were the records of the American Trotting Horse, of which the Morgan was then considered a family. He also consulted the *American Saddle Horse Register* where much of the foundation stock was Morgan or part Morgan.

OFFICIALLY A BREED

The publication of Volume I which gave a history of the breed for the first one hundred years stimulated much interest and enthusiasm among admirers and breeders of Morgans of the period. The Colonel encouraged all Morgan owners to trace and register the pedigrees of their horses. So contagious was his enthusiasm and so rewarding were his efforts that they resulted in Volume II being published in 1905. This volume was a supplement to Volume I and included many new pedigrees. The work of Joseph Battell had begun to bear fruit, and

Judging matched teams at a Vermont State Fair.

GENERAL GIFFORD *and his get at the 1908 Vermont Fair.*

the Morgan was being preserved and perpetuated as a definite breed —not merely as an offshoot of another.

In 1909 several dedicated breeders and supporters of the Morgan horse called together as many owners as could come to a meeting, with the purpose of organizing a Morgan club. They met, sixty strong, on September 23, 1909, at the Vermont State Fair in White River Junction, Vermont. Here the purposes of The Morgan Horse Club were outlined and subscribed to by all. A president, Henry S. Wardner, and a secretary-treasurer, C. C. Stillman, were chosen at this time, with plans being made for a future meeting when a constitution and by-laws could be adopted.

Thirty-one attended the second meeting held at Hartford, Vermont, on November 27, 1909. The constitution and by-laws were subsequently voted in and the election of a board of fifteen governors and five vice-presidents took place.

Impact of the Club

For several years the newly organized club held an annual meeting at the Vermont State Fair. The meetings were paralleled by a great

Bob Morgan

Prince Charlie   *Noted stallions circa 1910.*   Scotland

Bobby B

FLYHAWK

UPWEY KING BENN

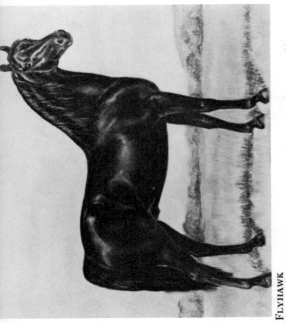

ORCLAND VIGILDON

CORNWALLIS

WINDCREST DONFIELD

PARADE

ORCLAND LEADER

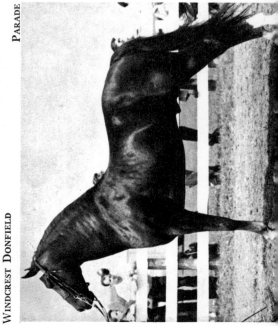

SEALECT OF WINDCREST

UPWEY BEN DON   Jeanne Mellin

showing of Morgan horses at each fair. In 1909, ninety were entered
for the show, but each year thereafter brought out added numbers of
fine animals until reportedly there were one hundred eighty entries
in 1914.

It seemed that the Morgan was on firm footing as a breed and on
its way, at last. Membership in the club reached a high point of 289
in 1914, with the majority of members residing in New England.

ULENDON   Clark Bayley

Many of those early members were men who had known Morgans all their lives, from the time when the Morgan held an enviable position on the harness tracks and during the period when they were popular and outstanding roadsters.

The 1917 meeting at the Vermont State Fair and its attendant fine showing of Morgans turned out to be the last one of its caliber for a number of years. However, after an absence of two years (during

World War I) when the meetings and the shows were resumed, nothing seemed the same and a drastic decline was in evidence from previous years. The automobile had honked the roadsters from the highways and the harness horse had followers only among the diehards. Only *five* members attended the annual meeting in White River in 1925, a far cry from the prewar days of 1914. It seemed then as though the Morgan had really come to the end of the road this time. Colonel Battell's tireless efforts on behalf of the breed had been terminated by his death in 1915 just as his third volume of the Morgan *Register* was about ready for publication.

The Register Revived

Middlebury College in Vermont, receiving the *Register* as part of Colonel Battell's estate, completed the publication of Volume III. Then C. C. Stillman, the original secretary-treasurer of The Morgan Horse Club and a noted breeder of Morgans, purchased the *Register* from the college and incorporated it as The American Morgan Horse Register, Inc., with Colonel Battell's works as the first three volumes. In Volume III all the stallions of the first three volumes were assigned numbers. It was also Mr. Stillman who published Volume IV in 1921. This volume included registrations recorded from about 1912 to 1920.

In 1921, which marked the one-hundredth anniversary of Justin Morgan's death, Mr. Stillman, personally bearing the full cost, presented to the United States Department of Agriculture the beautiful statue of Justin Morgan, in behalf of The Morgan Horse Club. The fine statue by sculptor Frederick Roth stands now, as it stood then, on the grounds of the Morgan Horse Farm in Weybridge, near Middlebury, Vermont.

Mr. Stillman died in August 1926 after having devoted so much of himself toward the perpetuation of the Morgan, and the club lost yet another dedicated admirer. He had not only carried on the work of the *Register* but had maintained offices for the club at his own expense in New York. His death left a great void, for the members had relied on Mr. Stillman to carry out much of the work of the club.

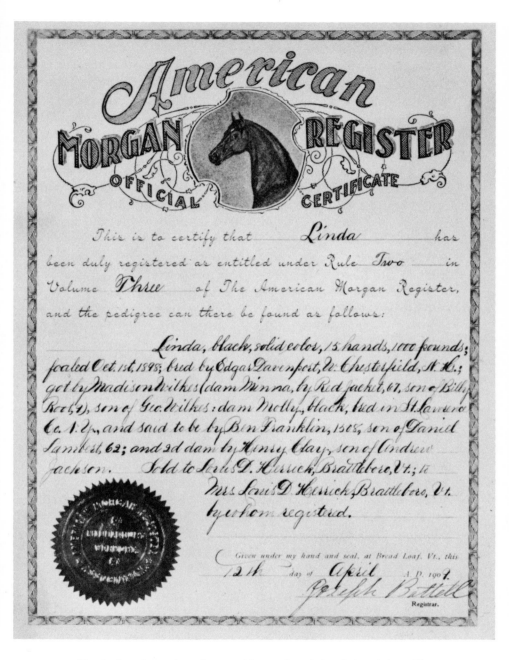

Typical early registration certificate signed by Colonel Battell.

Club and Register Combined

His successor, Charles A. Stone, along with the other directors, felt that the club should properly own and carry on its register—which until that time it had not done. Since the *Register* had been set up as a corporation and the club had no corporate entity, being only an informal society, it was necessary to incorporate the club before it could receive the assets of the *Register* from the Stillman estate.

In August 1927 at the regular annual meeting a plan, developed by Charles Stone, was presented to incorporate the Morgan club itself. Then with acceptance of the assets of the *Register* corporation, that corporation would be dissolved as such and would become a part of The Morgan Horse Club, Inc. A committee was formed and on November 1, 1927, the club became incorporated and subsequently the *Register* became an integral part of The Morgan Horse Club, Inc., and subject to control by the membership.

It was a few years after this took place that the breeding of Morgans fell to its lowest point. In 1933 there were only 78 registrations of horses and 63 transfers of ownership, and paid membership numbered only a scant 52. However a change for the better took place from the year 1934 on through World War II, when the general interest in pleasure riding gave many breeds of light horses the much-needed impetus.

In 1941 Charles Stone, who had been an active member and served as a director and officer since 1912, passed away, leaving yet another serious vacancy in the club roster. Like Mr. Stillman before him, Mr. Stone had also provided the club with office facilities in New York for the club work. Whitney Stone, club treasurer, followed the generous example of his father and continued to provide the offices for the club's business. Thereafter Frank B. Hills, secretary and registrar since 1931, continued to serve in this capacity until his passing in March 1961.

RIDING HIGH

By the early 1940s the Morgan breed had made huge strides. In 1941, 402 horses were registered, as compared with only 78 eight years earlier, and membership in the club had tripled. Interest in the breed was in evidence from many different parts of the country. By 1947 registrations reached their highest point since the club was founded, with 697 horses registered and membership up to almost three hundred. Each year since then has brought ever-increasing registrations and club activities.

The Magazine

A breed magazine was introduced by Owen Moon of Woodstock, Vermont, in 1941. An officer of the club, Mr. Moon published the first number, called the *Morgan Horse Bulletin,* at his own expense. With the fourth issue the name was changed to *The Morgan Horse Magazine.*

Mr. Moon published the magazine with success until his death in 1947, when the publication was presented to The Morgan Horse Club by Mrs. Moon. With news and pictures of Morgan activities and articles of interest about the breed, the magazine was and continues to be very instrumental in introducing the Morgan horse and his virtues to a wide audience.

The Local Groups

Today The Morgan Horse Club—with affiliated local clubs springing up all over America, and even one in Canada—has attained the position envisioned by its founders. With membership climbing from the dismal low of less than forty in 1927 to thirty-five hundred in 1960, the club and the breed have advanced enormously over the years.

For the benefit of present (and future) Morgan enthusiasts a list of clubs at the time of writing is given below.

The Morgan Horse Club, Inc.: Seth P. Holcombe, Secretary, P.O. Box 2157, Bishops Corner Branch, West Hartford, 17, Connecticut

The New York State Morgan Horse Society, Inc.: Miss Nancy Gochee, Corresponding Secretary, Turin Road, Rome, New York

New England Morgan Horse Association: Mrs. Seth Holcombe, Secretary, 57 E. Weatogue Street, Simsbury, Connecticut

Maine Morgan Horse Club: Miss Janet McGovern, Secretary, Route 1, West Scarboro, Maine

Mid-Atlantic Morgan Horse Club: Miss Helene Zimmerman, Secretary, Box 98, Maple Glen, Pennsylvania

Justin Morgan Horse Association: Edgar Mansfield, Secretary-Treasurer, 33636 Hillcrest Drive, Farmington, Michigan

Connecticut Morgan Horse Association: Mrs. Ellsworth Wollcott, Secretary, Bloomfield, Connecticut

Mid-America Morgan Horse Club: Mrs. George Norton, Secretary, R.F.D. 2, Monroe, Wisconsin

Kyova (Kentucky-Ohio-West Virginia) Morgan Horse Association: Mrs. H. E. West, Secretary-Treasurer, Route 1, Parkersburg, West Virginia

Mississippi Valley Morgan Horse Club: Mrs. William C. Byers, Secretary-Treasurer, 11057 Breezy Point, St. Louis, Missouri

The Indiana Morgan Horse Club: Mrs. Rachel Centers, Secretary-Treasurer, R.R. 2, Portland, Indiana

Central States Morgan Horse Club, Inc.: LaVerne Miller, Secretary-Treasurer, Downers Grove, Illinois

North Central Morgan Association: Raymond G. Anderson, Corresponding Secretary, 1509 Tenth Street, South Fargo, North Dakota

Ohio Morgan Association: Mrs. A. J. Andreoli, Secretary-Treasurer, 3333 West Bath Road, Akron 13, Ohio

Circle J Morgan Horse Association: Mrs. Virginia Banta, Secretary-Treasurer, 3272 Woodland Road, Los Almos, New Mexico

Morgan Horse Association of Oregon: Lois Groshong, Secretary-Treasurer, Route 1, Box 207, Albany, Oregon

Northern California Morgan Horse Club: Mrs. Delno Norton, Secretary-Treasurer, 7910 Hembre Lane, Windsor, California

Pacific Northwest Morgan Horse Association: Mrs. Leo H. Beckley, Secretary-Treasurer, 307 South 11th Street, Mt. Vernon, Washington

The Morgan Horse Club of Southern California: Orval Smith, Secretary-Treasurer, 1223 South 10th Avenue, Arcadia, California

". . . the head should be clean cut . . . eyes large, dark and prominent . . . the ears carried alertly . . ."

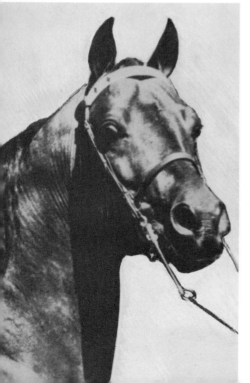
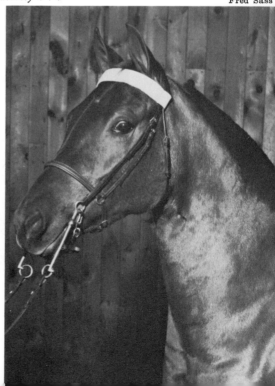

The success of The Morgan Horse Club and the local groups —indeed the growing popularity of the Morgan horse—can be said to owe much to the dedicated men who have stood by it these many years. Since the inception of the club these men have, through faith and affection for the Morgan, given of themselves in both time and money to support the club in all its efforts. We are all very much indebted to: Colonel Battell, whose lifelong research made possible the founding of the *Register;* to C. C. Stillman, through whose help The Morgan Horse Club was organized and Volume IV was published; and certainly to Charles A. Stone and his son, Whitney Stone, who reorganized the club for the purpose of ownership and perpetuation of the *Register.*

To quote the late Frank Hills, who served the club so well as secretary and registrar for many years: "With this foundation, future generations must certainly carry on the good work, endeavor to improve the breed of Morgan horses and widen the circle of those who will have pleasure in their ownership and use."

XII

The Morgan Horse Farm

AFTER the turn of the century, despite the efforts of a few dedicated breeders the Morgan horse was, as a breed, on extremely precarious footing. Indeed the Morgan was almost on the brink of extinction, being driven to the wall, as it were, by the advent of the automobile and the rise of the Standardbred horse. Therefore the government of the United States, maintaining an experiment station at Burlington, Vermont, to test the breeding and feeding of livestock, was urged to step in to try to save the Morgan.

The first suggestion that the Department of Agriculture take over this work was made by Senator Redfield Proctor, chairman of the Senate Committee on Agriculture in 1904. In the fall of 1905 the breeding of Morgans was arranged at the experiment station farm, and the first purchases of Morgan stock took place in June 1906 when a board of competent men acquired seven mares and two fillies to be used in the government's work; the mares were in foal when purchased or were bred immediately thereafter.

AS A FEDERAL VENTURE

The aim of the project at the time was to produce true Morgan type, with stress also on an increase in size and quality over that sometimes in evidence in the old Morgans. However type was to be adhered to and not sacrificed to size, as had happened previously. The department advertised for mares as follows:

"They should be from 5 to 8 years old, and standing 15.1-15.3 hands and weighing 1000-1150 pounds. Colors preferred: Brown, bay, chestnut. Grays not to be submitted for inspection unless exceptional individuals. Mares submitted for inspection should be sound,

207

with good conformation, style and action and a pure trotting gait. They should be well bred along Morgan lines, but registration in the American Morgan Horse Register will not be necessary."

It is interesting to note that the government considered the over-15-hand horse more desirable in the proposed breeding program despite the fact that many of the best examples of the early Morgans were under this height. This was soon to be a sore point with some of the old Vermont breeders, and they criticized the Department of Agriculture for what they considered failure to produce the true or "ancient" (as it was sometimes called) type.

Of the mares purchased in Vermont only three were not registered or eligible to be recorded in the Morgan *Register*. But the real trouble came when the Department of Animal Industry brought back from Kentucky two mares sired by the illustrious Harrison Chief, a registered American Saddlebred. Both mares through their dams traced to Morgan blood, however, and their purchase was an experiment to determine whether or not a careful outcross to the blood of Harrison Chief would produce the desired increase in size and the quality without loss of the Morgan type.

The uproar among Morgan breeders caused by the Kentucky purchase brought down upon the heads of the department much acid criticism. One comment was that the department was attempting to restore the Morgan by the same method that had been used to destroy it, namely the outcrossing to other blood. The department retaliated by pointing out that the bloodlines of the Kentucky mares were established from Morgan foundation stock brought to Kentucky from New England farms. They also argued that the outcross to Saddleblood was far different from the crossing to the Standardbred which was done earlier when speed was the sole objective and type was lightly considered, if at all. However the department was content to let the Kentucky experiment stand as planned.

The Move to Weybridge

In 1907, through the great generosity of Colonel Joseph Battell, the United States Government was presented with his four-hundred-acre Breadloaf Farm in Weybridge (near Middlebury), Vermont, for the perpetuation and improvement of the Morgan horse. The stock from the Vermont Experimental Station at Burlington was taken to the Battell farm in the latter part of 1907, and at the donor's request Breadloaf Farm became officially known as The United States Morgan Horse Farm. In 1908 Colonel Battell donated another tract of land adjoining the farm, and in 1917 nearly five hundred adjoining acres were purchased. Today the farm consists of 942.5 acres, divided into meadows, pastureland and woods. There are thirty-five buildings on the land and a half-million feet of timber.

General Gates and His Get

The foundation stud of the government farm was General Gates 666, foaled May 6, 1894, and bred by Colonel Battell. A black without any white markings, General Gates stood 14.3 hands, weighed 1,000 pounds and was a fine, impressive horse. He was sired by Denning Allen 74, a son of Honest Allen and a grandson of the great Ethan Allen 50. His dam was Fanny Scott, who was by the noted Thoroughbred Revenue Jr and out of a mare by the old Morgan, Copperbottom. A full brother to Lord Clinton, whose trotting record was 2:10¼, General Gates was the head of the government farm until he died in 1920.

Although admitted to be an excellent horse, General Gates was the object of much criticism because of his other-than-Morgan blood, the more vitriolic calling him a mongrel and no more than a half-bred Morgan. This reaction may have had some justification, but men of the time who were well acquainted with old Black Hawk 20 declared that General Gates resembled the famous son of Sherman Morgan to a remarkable degree. As far as the Thoroughbred cross in General Gates's pedigree is concerned, it needs little defense when you consider that, according to the best information available, Justin Morgan himself had much more Thoroughbred blood than General Gates and that even old Black Hawk's dam, as far as can be determined, was a "half-bred" mare.

The purchase of General Gates to head the government stud, despite the disparaging remarks made at the time, has proved to be a successful venture and few can deny at this later date that the work

U.S.D.A. Photograph

The statue of Justin Morgan, 1 A.M.R., was given to the farm the year after General Gates, 666 A.M.R., died: but here they are for comparison.

of The United States Morgan Horse Farm has been the backbone of Morgan horse production since the breeding program's inception. General Gates was purchased after much careful consideration and the selection was made not only because he himself was a fine individual of the modern Morgan type but also because his offspring possessed his outstanding conformation and were easily recognized as being sired by him. He epitomized the type of Morgan that the government felt would best suit the modern markets, where the demand had shifted somewhat from the harness to the saddle horse.

Some of the early Morgans had a tendency toward coarseness, with round withers and low backs. Unfortunately there also was in evidence a choppiness and irregularity of gait and occasionally a tendency to pace and mix gaits. The aim of the government farm was to attempt to eliminate these unfavorable characteristics of the breed while keeping its splendid conformation, spirit and endurance.

BENNINGTON

Probably General Gates's best-known son as far as today's breeders are concerned was Bennington 5693—although his son Red Oak 5249 and Linsley 7233 also figure prominently in Western Morgan pedigrees, as the former went to Texas under the ownership of Richard Sellman and the latter stood in Kansas.

Bennington, a bay foaled in 1908, was to become one of the most important factors in the government's line-breeding program. By General Gates and out of Mrs. Culvers (one of the mares purchased in Kentucky), he had his disparagers, because feeling was still much against the use of the Harrison Chief mare.

Harrison Chief was by Clark Chief 2993 (foaled 1861, bay, 16 hands) and was registered as a Trotting Horse. However because he showed tremendous quality, he subsequently became a star of the show rings of the time. His dam, Lute Boyd, was a fine little show mare and a great-great-granddaughter of the famous Sir Archy, one of the finest Thoroughbreds ever imported to this country. She was one of Kentucky's best show mares, winning many championships even at an early age. Lute Boyd was bred to Clark Chief three times: the first resulting in a rather disappointing bay stud foal and the

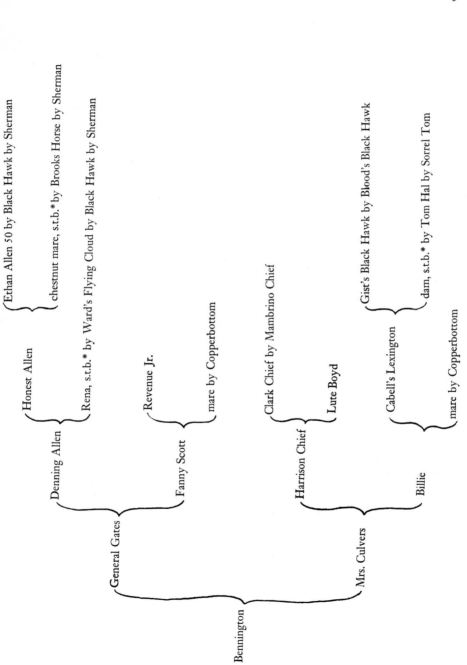

U.S.D.A. Photograph

BENNINGTON

second in a bay filly which became one of the great Saddlebred foundation mares; her third foal was Harrison Chief. This stallion, a beautiful blood-bay, had eight brilliant seasons in the ring shown always in harness; it is said that it was unlikely that he ever wore a saddle in his life.

Harrison Chief had an exceedingly successful record at stud, siring some of the best Saddlebreds of that or any time. As mentioned earlier, the well-known Bourbon Chief and the great show mare Lou Chief were among the countless names to bring fame to their sire. Mrs. Culvers, therefore, combining the blood of Harrison Chief and that of Cabell's Lexington (sired by Gist's Black Hawk, a son of Black Hawk 20, and registered both as a Morgan and as an Ameri-

U.S.D.A. Photograph

MANSFIELD

can Saddle Horse) through her dam brought to the Morgan breed a generous share of beauty and show ability. It was pointed out by those furthering the cause of the government's breeding program that much of the blood that produced Justin Morgan himself flowed richly in the veins of these Kentucky-bred horses. Even many of their critics who had found such fault with government ideas on breeding Morgans soon came around and later were known to have referred to the government Morgans as "the proper type."

MANSFIELD AND ETHAN ALLEN 3RD

Bennington was not used extensively at the government farm until 1925, having been used mainly in the military horse breeding pro-

ETHAN ALLEN 3RD

gram for twelve to fifteen years. It was after he stood at stud at the farm that many felt much valuable time was lost by not using this horse sooner. His first foals at Weybridge came up to expectations and were to be the foundation of the line-breeding program carried on by the government there for almost thirty years. Bennington and his outstanding son Mansfield 7255 were both used extensively until the mid-'30s when Mansfield carried on alone as the leading sire. This great chestnut headed the stud for twenty years and won championships virtually every time he was shown, as well as siring some of the most outstanding Morgans ever produced there.

Mansfield was foaled in 1920. One of the Morgan horse farm's most highly esteemed stallions in the opinion of just about everyone, he was out of Artemisia (chestnut, foaled 1909) who was by Ethan Allen 3rd. His dam's bloodlines show old Vermont breeding at its

Ethan Allen 3rd (Borden's), foaled 1885

- **(Peters') Ethan Allen 2nd**
  - **Peters' Morgan**
    - **Vermont**
      - **Jennie**
        - Hale's Green Mountain 42 by Gifford by Woodbury by Justin Morgan
        - Phoebe by Tom Morgan (Perkins Horse)
      - **chestnut mare**
        - Morgan Hunter 2nd by Morgan Hunter by Gifford by Woodbury by Justin Morgan
        - bay mare by General Hibbard by Woodbury by Justin Morgan
    - **chestnut mare**
      - **Ethan Allen 50**
        - Black Hawk 20 by Sherman by Justin Morgan
        - gray mare by Red Robin, s.t.b.* by Justin Morgan
      - **chestnut mare**
        - Hale's Green Mountain 42 by Gifford by Woodbury by Justin Morgan
        - dark chestnut mare, s.t.b.* by Tom Morgan (Perkins Horse)
  - **chestnut mare**
- **bay mare**
  - **Cushings' Green Mountain**
    - **Hale's Green Mountain 42**
      - Gifford by Woodbury by Justin Morgan
      - bay mare, breeding unknown
    - **bay mare**
      - Billy Root by Sherman by Justin Morgan
      - Crane mare, s.t.b.* by Sherman by Justin Morgan
  - **brown mare**
    - **Charlie Watson**
      - **Black Morgan**
        - Green Mountain by Sherman by Justin Morgan
        - gray mare by Wilder's colt by Batchelder Horse by Sherman by Justin Morgan
      - **chestnut mare**
        - Comet by Billy Root by Sherman by Justin Morgan
        - **bay mare**
          - Wilson Horse by Royal Morgan by Sherman by Justin Morgan
          - bay mare by Batchelder Horse by Sherman by Justin Morgan
    - **brown mare**
      - Tiger by Baldwin's Black Hawk by Black Hawk 20 by Sherman by Justin Morgan
      - bay mare by Dr. Abel Brown Horse by Billy Root by Sherman by Justin Morgan

*said to be

best, for she traced in male line to Hale's Green Mountain Morgan and Gifford Morgan, and her dam was by Bob Morgan (by Ethan Allen 2nd), a stallion of excellent type and breeding. Ethan Allen 3rd (Borden's) was by Ethan Allen 2nd and out of a granddaughter of old Green Mountain Morgan. He was described by one of his owners as having a remarkably gentle disposition and his style and action were likened to a Hackney. This same style and action have come down through this line of breeding to the present day. A son of Ethan Allen 3rd, Sir Ethan Allen 6537, was twice Grand Champion Morgan Stallion at the Vermont State Fair, and his son Sealect was reserve to him there in 1922. Cornwallis, a son of Sealect, displayed the same high-headed, sprightly action of this line.

QUERIDO, ULYSSES AND CANFIELD

Mansfield's full brothers, Querido 7370, Ulysses 7565 and Canfield 7788, went on to make names for themselves as well, and their get were in great demand the country over, such was their excellence. As mentioned in a previous chapter, Querido, foaled in 1923, went to California and has gone down in Morgan history as the sire of qualified stock horses. He was used for many years by Roland Hill on his Horse-Shoe Cattle Company Ranch; and Sonfield, by Mansfield out of Quietude by Troubadour of Willowmoor, followed Querido in producing working stock horses for ranch use.

Ulysses, foaled in 1927 and Grand Champion in 1932 and 1939, if he had done nothing more than sire the great Ulendon 7831, would still have his niche in the Morgan Hall of Fame. Ulendon, the black stallion foaled in 1933, has been a champion himself and the sire and grandsire of champion after champion down to the present day. Orland Leader, out of Vigilda Burkland, and his full brother, Orcland Vigildon—Grand Champions in their own right—are two of Ulendon's outstanding sons. One could go on to great lengths describing the show records chalked up by the sons and daughters of old Ulendon in recent years.

Canfield was foaled in 1932 and although not the sire of so lengthy a list of champions, had the Grand Champion Stallion Pan-

Sealect breeding.

field to his credit, who in turn sired the Grand Champion Mare, Symphonee. Panfield is being used at the present time in the breeding program of the University of Connecticut. Many of Canfield's progeny have been noted for their fine gaits and endurance.

Results Achieved

The Morgans bred at the government farm have repeatedly met the demands of breeders and single buyers alike. Their varied abilities have proved the worth of their background and pedigree. Almost every important breeder of Morgans in the country has horses of government farm bloodlines and it is certainly safe to say that whether pro or con, General Gates, Bennington, Mansfield and their get are stallions who have had a marked effect on the Morgan of today.

On the bridle path and trail, government-farm-bred Morgans have racked up impressive records through the years. In the records of the old 300-Mile Endurance Rides and the 100-Mile Trail Ride in Woodstock, Vermont, the names of farm-bred Morgans appear frequently. Old Castor 5833, an 800-pound son of General Gates, made quite a reputation for himself in the early '20s on the endurance rides, as did the gelding Gladstone 6922, his paternal half-brother.

Mansfield's get in later years also carried high the government

CANFIELD   U.S.D.A. Photograph

farm banner: Friendly, by Mansfield out of a Bennington mare, won the Lightweight Division of the 100-Mile Trail Ride in 1942 and '43; and Lippitt Morman, out of the well-known mare Lippitt Kate Moro, became the first stallion to win a division of the ride: he won the Heavyweight in 1945 and the following year the Sweepstakes. Cassandra, another mare by Mansfield, also was an outstanding trail-ride contestant.

In the show ring the records of government farm Morgans are too numerous to list here, for all through the years the Weybridge-bred horses have showered the farm with honors. It is easy to see from the many winnings of Troubadour of Willowmoor 6459, to the Morgans that carry on today—Panfield, Mentor, Tutor and Cantor, to mention only a few—that the government farm blood has perpetuated outstanding Morgans and so has kindled the public's interest in a breed that had come dangerously close to disappearing.

MENTOR

TUTOR

Earl Krantz as Superintendent

The superintendent of the government farm for a great many years until his retirement in June 1951 was Earl B. Krantz, a veteran horseman of the United States Department of Agriculture. A native of Nebraska, Mr. Krantz was graduated from Iowa State College in 1915 with a degree in animal husbandry and received a Master of Science degree in this subject from Washington State College the following year. Research work with horses in Washington, D.C., Laramie, Wyoming, and Miles City, Montana, culminated in his taking the post at the Morgan farm in April 1928.

He was recognized as a national authority on horses, especially the light breeds, and managed the Weybridge farm so capably that it was brought to a point of international recognition, attracting widespread interest among Morgan breeders. Always maintaining that the modern Morgan must be bred for the saddle to be suitable for present-day demands, Mr. Krantz spent his years on the farm developing the breeding program which has successfully produced Morgans with size, ability and endurance while preserving type. That this breeding program has had a dominant influence on Morgan horse production throughout the country can be seen by the number of Morgans of government farm breeding which are carry-

CANTOR

ing on in the show ring, on the trail and at stud.

In 1941 under Mr. Krantz's direction the Bureau of Animal Industry began conducting performance tests on three-year-old Morgans for the purpose of determining the characteristics associated with performance, and whether these characteristics are inherited and can therefore be used in the selection of breeding stock. The object of the experiment, carried on for ten years, was to correlate the horse's physique with its ability to do useful work.

The three types of performance studied were speed, endurance and ease of riding. Many characteristics were measured or scored for each horse so that associations between them and performance could be determined. Under his direction sixty-eight three-year-old Morgans, raised and trained on the farm, were used in this experiment. They were sired by eight different stallions and ranged from two to twenty-five offspring per sire. Included among these were six stallions, twenty geldings and forty-two mares.

Fascinating results were obtained from these tests, which were scored on general conformation, style and beauty, quality and other characteristics; action at the walk and trot, as well as endurance, recuperative powers and comfort to the rider at various gaits. The relationship between conformation and various other desirable characteristics was measured and recorded under Mr. Krantz's direction. The results were valuable to all light-horse breeds.

VERMONT TAKES OVER

Despite all the good work accomplished by The United States Morgan Horse Farm, the government in December 1950 voted to discontinue funds for the farm's operation at the end of the fiscal year. Funds were offered and provided by private sources until the legislature of the State of Vermont could consider a proposal for the state to take over the farm.

In January 1951, after the General Assembly of Vermont had decided in favor of continuing the operation, a dispersal was ordered because the state did not choose to maintain the complete herd. Reserving twenty mares and four stallions to be used on the farm, which was to be run by the University of Vermont and the State College of Agriculture, the other stock—eleven mares and sixteen stallions—were offered to the public for sale by sealed bid. However four Eastern universities were granted horses to aid in their respective Morgan breeding programs. They were:

University of Massachusetts, eleven mares and fillies and two stallions;

RIVIERA

University of Connecticut, four mares and one stallion;
University of New Hampshire, two mares, and
University of Pennsylvania, two mares.

When the 398 bids were opened on January 3, 1951, it was obvious that the public was well impressed by Morgans of government farm breeding, if the prices these horses brought were any indication. The top-priced horse of the sale was the good three-year-old mare Riviera, a daughter of Mentor, who went to Nelson White for $2,525. Another daughter of Mentor, a four-year-old named Quakerlady, brought $1,751, and went to Pennsylvania State College. Panfield, among the stallions, went to Kansas for the price of $1,600.

The United States Government officially turned over the farm to the University of Vermont on July 1, 1951, and this institution has successfully continued the work to which Mr. Krantz devoted so much of his life and talents.

Students at UVM—as the university is called—work with, feed, fit and show the Morgans. In addition, annual Morgan Horse Judging Schools have been held at Weybridge since 1954 for the benefit of horse lovers, breeders and professional judges. Riding clubs and 4-H light-horse groups also come for information to the farm, whose demonstrations have proved of great value to the area. Besides all these dyed-in-the-wool fanciers, many thousands of people from all over the country have visited the farm to see the Morgans.

More Records

With UVM management the farm has continued its winning ways at the shows as well as in the production of fine Morgans. Charles Gerry, head horseman in whose capable hands the farm's thirty-five horses are thriving so well, has trained and exhibited a number of his charges to important wins in state and regional shows as well as in the National itself. Under him UVM Cantor was Reserve Grand Champion Stallion at the 1959 National and Tutor, a son of Mentor, won the coveted Get-of-Sire Class at the show the same year.

Other outstanding Morgans at the farm today include Symphonee, (Panfield-Inez) the Grand Champion Mare at the 1951 National who heads the band of twenty broodmares, and Norma, a daughter of

University of Massachusetts mares.

Washington, D.C., in snow provides a made-to-order background for these typy

Canfield. Also outstanding is UVM Flash (a coming three-year-old by Upwey Ben Don), who was top yearling at the National and every other competition entered in 1959. UVM Cantor, the lovely young chestnut son of Tutor, is well on his way to being an outstanding sire as well as show horse, for his colts are showing a great deal of promise even at this early date. There is also Inez (Delmont-Topaz); and not to be forgotten is old Fairytop, dam of Mentor, who at twenty-five years of age has produced seventeen living foals!

More Interest

Although the show records and the scores of ribbons hanging in the barn office indicate the farm's avid interest in the exhibition of their stock, nevertheless the production of pleasure horses is equally important. The Morgan endurance and disposition is evidently known on a world-wide scale among horsemen, as buyers from as far afield as Peru, China, Puerto Rico and Israel have had Morgans shipped to their respective countries. In 1947 Magellen, a government-farm stallion, headed a group of twenty-five Morgans to be shipped across the sea to Nationalist China to bolster the cavalry stock there. What became of the horses after the fall of the mainland to the Communists is anybody's guess, but it is reported that two of the Morgans were recognized during the Korean War—and that one of them was Magellen, being ridden by a Chinese Communist general: a strange fate for a Yankee stallion from New England!

...rebred Morgans, pride of the United States Park Police.   Harry Naltchayan—Washington Post Photo

Less remote is the use of Morgans for police work, especially where mounted officers are "on show." This equable, competent and striking breed is represented on several metropolitan police forces, including the United States Park Police in the nation's capital.

The demands for Morgans pour into the office of the farm at Weybridge in increasing numbers as the years go by, valid proof that the work of the federal goverment in perpetuating the breed and the continuing efforts of the University of Vermont have been greatly appreciated and highly successful. To quote Donald J. Balch, assistant professor of animal husbandry: "We cannot begin to satisfy the calls for Morgans, though we raise from twelve to fifteen colts a year, and the demand for mature animals which are trained or even partially trained is tremendous."

Both Professor Balch and Luther Kinney, the farm's present superintendent, are optimistic about the farm's future although at times recently it looked as if the State of Vermont would vote to discontinue it. Letters of encouragement and enthusiasm for the farm's value to the College of Agriculture as well as to the Morgan breed poured in from all parts of the country in hopes to dissuade the legislators from abandoning the operation of the farm. It is fervently hoped that soon continuation will be definitely and permanently assured—especially since the 1961 General Assembly voted to make the Morgan horse Vermont's official state animal.

Meanwhile the heroic statue of Justin Morgan, symbol of years of Morgan horse breeding at Weybridge, stands above the sweeping green fields where foals in its image play beside their dams. The neat white barn which rang with the hoofbeats of General Gates and

Bennington and Mansfield, bears on its worn wooden floors the im-
prints of newer champions. And it is the earnest wish of Morgan admirers everywhere that the sound of horses' feet will never cease to
echo in the shadow of their patriarch, Justin Morgan.

HOME FARMS OF LIVING CHAMPIONS

PICTURED IN THE TEXT

BIG BILL B: owned by Mrs. John Junk, Sugar Run Farm, Mount Sterling, Ohio

CANTOR: owned by University of Vermont Morgan Horse Farm, Weybridge, Vermont

GEORGE GOBEL: owned by Mr. and Mrs. Wm. W. Barton, Big Bend Farms, Rockford, Illinois

JOHN GEDDES: owned by Mr. and Mrs. Walter Kane, Woods and Water Farms, South Lyon, Michigan

U.C. MENTION: owned by Mr. and Mrs. Gordon Voorhis, Voorhis Farm, Red Hook, New York

MENTOR: owned by University of Connecticut, Storrs, Connecticut

ORCLAND LEADER: owned by Mr. and Mrs. Stephen Tompkins, Bar-T Farm, Rowley, Massachusetts

ORCLAND VIGILDON: owned by Mr. and Mrs. Roger Ela, Townshend Morgan-Holstein Farm, Bolton, Massachusetts

PARADE: owned by Mr. and and Mrs. J. Cecil Ferguson, Broadwall Farm, Greene, Rhode Island

RIVIERA: owned by Mr. Joseph Hoyt, Chillicothe, Ohio

SEALECT OF WINDCREST: owned by Mr. and Mrs. Gordon Voorhis, Voorhis Farm, Red Hook, New York

SONFIELD: owned by Mr. Leo Beckley, Mount Vernon, Washington

TUTOR: owned by University of Vermont Morgan Horse Farm, Weybridge, Vermont

ULENDON: owned by Mr. and Mrs. Wallace Orcutt Jr, Orcland Farms, West Newbury, Massachusetts

UPWEY BEN DON: owned by Mrs. F. O. Davis, Wind-Crest Farm, Windsor, Vermont

UPWEY KING BENN: owned by Mr. Stuart G. Hazard, Topeka, Kansas

WINDCREST DONA LEE: owned by Mrs. Antoinette Kelley, Buttonwood Farm, Chester, Vermont

WINDCREST DONFIELD: owned by Mrs. D. D. Power, Waseeka Farm, Ashland, Massachusetts

Index

233